THE TOOTH FAIRY

THE

ALSO BY CLIFFORD CHASE

The Hurry-Up Song: A Memoir of Losing My Brother
Queer 13: Lesbian and Gay Writers Recall Seventh Grade (editor)
Winkie

TOOTH FAIRY

PARENTS, LOVERS, AND OTHER WAYWARD DEITIES
(A MEMOIR)

Clifford Chase

The Overlook Press
NEW YORK, NY

This edition first published in hardcover in the United States in 2014 by
The Overlook Press, Peter Mayer Publishers, Inc.

141 Wooster Street
New York, NY 10012
www.overlookpress.com
For bulk and special sales, please contact sales@overlookny.com,
or write us at the address above.

Library of Congress Cataloging-in-Publication Data

Chase, Clifford.
Tooth fairy : parents, lovers, and other wayward deities : a memoir
/ Clifford Chase. — First edition.
pages cm
1. Chase, Clifford. 2. Authors, American—21st century—
Biography. I. Title.
PS3603.H3793Z46 2014 818'.603—dc23 [B] 2013043498

Book design and type formatting by Bernard Schleifer
Manufactured in the United States of America
ISBN: 978-1-4683-0695-8

First Edition
1 3 5 7 9 10 8 6 4 2

For John

Out there
a bird is building a nest out of torn up letters . . .

—JAMES SCHUYLER, "An East Window on Elizabeth Street"

THE TOOTH FAIRY

1

FAT LITTLE DOG trotting contentedly along the sidewalk, right at his master's side, with a plastic steak in his mouth.

"Neil Young sounds like a lonely alley cat," I thought, "most poignant when slightly out of tune."

Whenever I got on the subway, I looked around for someone cute to glance at, and if there wasn't anyone I resigned myself to boredom.

Old queen in the locker room: "When you're the prettiest one in the steam room, it's time to go home."

At forty-three I was no longer in my heyday.

The name of the medication printed in a half circle and the "100 mg" made a smiley face on my new, blue pills.

On the L train, a poem called "Hunger" spoke of walking home "through a forest that covers the world."

I'd had the same part-time public-relations job since November 1985. It was now February 2001 and counting.

I was drawn to Neil Young not by the specific content of the lyrics (too hetero) but by the overall tone of longing, which I defined as a kind of sadness that had hope.

On the L platform, a diminutive Chinese man playing "Send in the Clowns" on a harmonica, to flowery recorded accompaniment.

I write this in the hope that aphorism-like statements, when added one to another, might accrue to make some larger statement that will placate despair.

"The intensity of certain random experiences," I wrote in my journal, "is sometimes unaccountable and makes one wish to live more observantly."

I'd hoped to overcome negative thinking through therapy, meditation, prayer, swimming, and yoga, but now it appeared I also needed a drug.

According to WebMD, Wellbutrin carries a risk of seizure.

Thought: The problem with polyester is that it pills, yet sometimes it doesn't, and you can never tell which it will be.

After eight years together John and I still didn't share an apartment, and I wondered if this was a failure.

"Let the seizure come," I thought, "and maybe afterwards I'll have some peace."

I supported myself mostly with public-relations writing and

only sometimes with journalism, because public-relations writing is always positive, and I like to be nice.

In his spare time, my ophthalmologist was an amateur magician.

I went to look at the sunset and was given a ticket for trespassing.

My arthritis was bad that week, but I hoped that if I thought of myself as a well person rather than a sick one, the pain would bother me less and less and might even go away.

"Colors were brighter," said a woman of her first week on Effexor, which I had also tried but didn't like.

My Walkman in my breast pocket, I floated along with the sad tune.

The ronroco, a small Argentine string instrument, sounds like a cross between a ukulele and a mandolin.

In an e-mail regarding the freelance article I was working on, the marketing executive at Jordache tried to flirt with me by offering vintage jeans and asking my waist size.

Journal: "I like Internet porn too much."

John and I enjoyed how Mae West makes odd, inarticulate, knowing "humph" sounds, sometimes barely audible, and when she "dances," she barely moves.

I wrote that the old 1979 Jordache commercial, which was being shown again on TV, "begins with a downward glissando," a line my editor took out, even though that glissando is my favorite part of the ad.

Joni Mitchell once wisely observed that disco music "sounds like typewriters."

My editor also cut: "We only glimpse the blond girl dancing, in a manner not seen since, say, the New York City Gay Pride Parade in 1989, that is, as if her shoulders are attached to one circular track and her hips to another."

I noticed that whenever I trimmed my sideburns, I thought of a particular editor I barely knew, and since I liked her, I didn't mind thinking of her while shaving, but sometimes I asked myself, why her?

For another article, I spent my day off in Staten Island interviewing once again the teenager with HIV I had interviewed two and a half years earlier.

Noelle, my therapist of twelve years, almost started crying as she spoke of another patient, a priest, who had died of AIDS.

I went in search of a black version of the navy blue cotton-polyester polo shirt I'd seen at Bloomingdale's, and I found it at Saks.

Though my brother had died of AIDS and we had discussed this many times, I had never seen Noelle cry before.

As soon as I switched from Effexor to Wellbutrin, my orgasm returned.

"The colors of some moments are slightly brighter than

others," I wrote, "and some a lot brighter, and at the moment I'm interested in those just slightly brighter."

I told John how much I love blood oranges.

I went home and tried on all my new clothes.

John said I'm like that dog with his plastic steak when I have a new shirt to wear.

Articles I might have written for *GQ:* "Searching for the Perfect Black Polo Shirt"; "Shoe Shopping With My Podiatrist"; "How Can You Tell If a Particular Polyester Blend Will Pill?"; "Why Do Certain Flat-Front Pants Wrinkle So Much in the Crotch?"

I was thinking of leaving Noelle and even went to see three new candidates but decided I would just reach the same point with a new one eventually, for reasons that are officially known as "resistance" and "transference," and which in practical terms meant I was afraid to go forward.

My mother and father liked to playfully call milk "malk" and cooking "coo-king."

Similarly, John and I repeat the same phrases again and again, phrases from movies or life that made us laugh, as when John overheard a fag in a coffee shop say, apparently of his boyfriend, "I don't know *where* she is, I don't know if she's got a *dick* in her mouth . . ."

Thought: When you feel a strong connection to your therapist, you not only mistake her for your mother, but she sort of really *is* your mother, because she has taught you as much as a mother would.

In an e-mail, my friend Cathy, who is legally blind, explained to me for the first time in our twenty-two-year friendship exactly what she sees—that is, a rapid series of blurry snapshots, because her eyes won't hold still.

I begged off having a drink with my boss, saying I had dinner plans, which was true: I had planned to have dinner with myself.

I said I couldn't have lunch with the salespeople tomorrow because there was something I had to do, which was true: I had to be alone.

Things I liked to do on Wellbutrin: blow my boyfriend; lie in bed switching channels; write one-sentence paragraphs; not get mad at store clerks; masturbate; read stereo-equipment catalogs; plan to go to Rome.

Soaked through after walking only half a block, I said to myself, "This weather is absurd. Absurd!"

I was discouraged to discover that certain childhood experiences continued to wreck my life, and so I had to look at them one more time.

Subway grafitti: "Admit when your gay and a slacker."

For five years I'd been writing a novel about my teddy bear, in part because I was (and am) perpetually in need of comfort.

Driving me back to the ferry, the grandmother of the kid with HIV said wryly, as we passed the hospital, "There it is, our home away from home."

When Noelle nearly cried, I said that maybe she was too fragile to be my therapist, but she replied that that wasn't the case.

On the telephone John and I tried to imitate Mae West's inarticulate humphs, but since they're nearly inaudible, we didn't have much success.

When I took my trespassing ticket to 346 Broadway, they said I had come on the wrong day.

In Union Square station, a teen to a fellow teen: "You sound like a fucking hibernating bear. Maybe you should sleep six months and shit."

"Moments of a certain off flavor add up," I wrote, "and then you perceive you're in a new phase of your life."

In my teddy-bear novel I would have to write about shitting my pants all the time when I was five, and I wasn't sure how to go about describing that.

After eight years, I related to John very well within certain parameters, and we were working to expand those parameters, but sometimes I was afraid I wasn't up to the challenge and couldn't change.

His nickname for me: Kid. My nickname for him: Kid.

My dentist pointed to a small dark area on the X-ray.

On the phone John read me a funny article about Kathy Lee Gifford.

"There are certain moments and facts the mind returns to, for whatever reason," I wrote.

I stared out my office window.

There was nothing more to be done for the tooth, so I would have to have it pulled, and it would have to done now, before I went to Rome.

Young subway cop, tubby and all in blue, standing by the token booth vigorously chewing his nails.

Thought: Didn't Dante refer to middle age as a "forest"?

*

"You may hear a cracking sound," said the oral surgeon, who was also named Cliff. He was inserting a pair of pliers in my mouth. I heard the cracking. Occasionally life plunges you into an experience that, for its utter intensity and obscure resonance, may as well be a dream. "You doin' okay?" Cliff asked. "Uh-huh," I tried to say, though actually even after the five or six shots of Novocain I still had some sensation in one spot on my gum, but this was too difficult to explain. My mouth was propped open by a black plastic brace, which I bit down on with my left teeth, the side he wasn't working on. Cliff said, "You're going to feel some vibration." I glimpsed the instrument before it went in. I wondered if he wished I'd opted for the Valium and Demerol, so that he wouldn't have to explain everything he was doing. He was, however, very good at explaining. I felt the high-pitched vibration of the power tool (drill? tiny saw?). Then the tugging of the pliers, as the gray-haired German-accented assistant gently but firmly—Germanly, I thought—held my chin in place. More tugging. This went on for a while, the power tool, then the pliers, first one root, then the other. I kept my eyes closed and the light on my eyelids was bright as daylight. I tried to imagine I was at the beach. Again and again my shoulders tensed up and I would have to remember to relax them. To describe this ordeal as primal might be misleading, since I was too deep in the woods of it to describe it to myself at all. If I were to interpret, I might say it confirmed a nameless and fundamental conviction that life had stolen something nameless and fundamental from me. This might also be called the human condition, but like the protagonist in a dream I was exempt, for the time being, from drawing any such conclusions. At last there was a final tug, which, though I could see nothing, seemed decisive and was. He dropped the pliers in the metal tray with a clang.

*

Just as I switched the channel to Jenny Jones, she said, "So, you have sex for money. And you work at White Castle?"

Mouth full of gauze, I had to stop by the office because the goddamn FedEx package hadn't arrived the day before.

On the subway stairs: "If I hear any more about your anger management class, I'm going to throw up."

I read that a fever after a tooth extraction is normal.

I began seeing flashing lights on the periphery of my left eye, so I called my magician-ophthalmologist, who told me I had Moore's Lightning Streaks, a harmless condition that can affect nearsighted people in middle age.

Apparently Barbara Stanwyck once said "Fuck you" to Loretta Young.

I tried to participate in my oral surgeon's manful matter-of-factness, but I still mourned the molar, designated "number 30."

I broke down when Noelle said she felt outrage for certain things I had suffered as a child.

Cliff had also been my oral surgeon more than fifteen years earlier, on this very same tooth, which that time was saved, and that time I did choose the Valium and Demerol—

"Cliff . . . Cliff . . . Cliff . . .? Howyadoin'?"

2

THOUGHT IN ROME: Perfectly cooked squid is like an extra-firm mattress for the teeth.

"I didn't realize it would be so tarted up," said John in the ancient church that had been redone in the Baroque style.

"I love *La Dolce Vita* because rather than making Marcello reform or 'find himself,'" I wrote, "it allows him simply to go further into depravity."

"They're so tall!" I said of the many sycamores, which were just getting their leaves.

After a week my tongue grew accustomed to the gap in my molars, and even began to caress the gap's edges lovingly.

"That meal will go down in history," I said, taking one last bite.

In exchange for the tooth, I had at least been granted the vivid experience of losing it.

Coming down through the billowing mosaic-clouds: God's hand.

As we ate our gelato, we decided we liked Rome better than Paris.

Journal: "Any single moment could be definitive and final, just as the world might end at any moment."

On our archeological tour beneath St. Peter's, the Vatican guide informed us that the early Christians depicted Jesus as the sun: "They didn't know what he looked like then, because that was, of course, before the Shroud of Turin."

I leaned against the refrigerator and it moved, prompting me to remark that Italian refrigerators are lighter than American ones.

Even on vacation John had moments of panicky sadness that I found at once understandable and terrifying.

At dinner we couldn't remember what calculus was, and I said it had something to do with describing a curve with an infinite number of separate points.

In the Vatican Museums, just after the Sistine Chapel, there was a small wooden box marked "Suggestions."

Pouting near the Coliseum, I was reminded strongly of childhood and thought to myself, "Whatever it is I'm feeling, it's very old, so why don't I just put it aside for now?," and somehow I was able to do just that.

"I like that game that Gary and Jean played, 'What City Would You Want to Live in If You Could Live Anywhere?'" I said to John, "though I have a feeling they play that game a lot," and John said, "So do we."

As a child I felt only excruciating embarrassment, rather than mirth, when the Beaver got into various scrapes, such as climbing up into a giant teacup on a billboard.

The stairs to our sleeping loft were metal and not very steep, and they clanged cheerfully as we quickly ascended and descended.

In the Caravaggio that made me understand Caravaggio, Doubting Thomas places his finger in the wound in Christ's side, and that wound is like a tear in the painting itself.

John laughed as I sang for him my new favorite song:

> *Papa was a rodeo*
> *Mama was a rock 'n' roll band*
> *I could play guitar and rope a steer*
> *Before I learned to stand*
> *Home was anywhere with diesel gas*
> *Love was a trucker's hand . . .*

Because the church's ceiling was being replastered, Michelangelo's famous sculpture of Moses had been covered in bubble wrap.

The pervasive, calming, cheerful sun.

We realized the delicious sandwiches we had just bought were only a dollar fifty.

"If a child will try to adjust to anything, including and especially parental failings," I wrote, "then I, too, played guitar and roped a steer before I learned to stand."

". . . bla bla bla Catherine Zeta-Jones bla bla bla," said the Italian television announcer.

The oranges we bought each day were large, sweet and just slightly bloody inside.

Bernini's elephant in sunshine.

At the gay-owned shop I bought John a cunning little pepper grinder for his birthday.

Our two bunches of ranunculuses lasted the whole nine days.

On the way to the airport the trees streamed past the train window as if they were being sucked up by a vacuum cleaner.

To sit on the aisle, I accepted a seat way in the back, but then the people next to me kept wanting to get up.

I found the in-flight movie almost unbearable because of the many humiliations suffered by the main character.

Journal: "The sky really does look different everywhere you go."

3

IN FIFTH GRADE I wrote an essay that concluded, "As Plato said, power corrupts."

"I don't know how much longer I can last in corporate America," I muttered, but then I'd been saying that for years.

I read that singer-songwriter Nick Drake killed himself with an overdose of amitriptyline; remembered that was the scientific name for what I'd been taking for arthritis pain; realized I had options.

On the record albums of my youth, the various aesthetic choices seemed so inevitable that they hardly appeared to be choices at all, such as when the applause following "The Needle and the Damage Done" is suddenly cut short.

I hoped that with the help of my blue pills I would either cease hating my public-relations job or be able to find a new one.

On the weather map the clouds were in a slow spin across the continent.

"The Long and Winding Road" had made me cry when I was twelve, and ever since then I had loved sad songs.

Without understanding why, that winter I had spiraled down into punishing sadness and terror, which manifested themselves most mercilessly on weekday evenings.

"Most jobs are nothing more than service with a smile, and then the day is over," I wrote.

People have often told me, "You're the only one I'm not mad at."

I wrote, "I can only deal with crying every other therapy session."

As I sank further, I became overwhelmed by even the smallest thing, a state which reminded me of my mother on a bad day.

I felt guilty when I snapped at customer service representatives, but I did it anyway.

I posited a magazine called *Naked GQ*, which would be exactly the same as *GQ*, only the models would all be naked.

Thought: The only problem with my blue pills, as with vacations, is that the same conundrums of work and love remain.

I frequently imagined screaming arguments with my boss and with others in management.

I was reading a book by a hunchback dwarf who died in 1942.

At the party celebrating his twentieth anniversary with the large magazine where I worked, the editor-in-chief said, "I tell my kids that if you can find a line of work that you love, then you're truly blessed," and I wrote it down to put in the company newsletter.

Ashamed of my life, including the shame itself.

"And yet I can also see glimmerings of some sort of perspective," I told Noelle.

After I wired John money in Tunisia, because his bankcard didn't work, I thought, "This is the kind of crisis I'm good at."

I was able to see the possible literary merit, if not the actual merit, of my predicament in life.

Journal: "I've always loved best works of art that are both absurd and moving."

A coworker told me a top executive had complained to her that there weren't enough blueberries in his muffin.

Riding the subway home from work I longed to hear Joni sing of being a poor wayfaring stranger.

At least it was spring.

The magazine's writers had recently published books on: baldness; civil rights; cryptography; early American music; an incident of arson in Vail, Colorado; current social and political issues (from a neocon perspective); and how to live "a happy life."

"Major quitting fantasies," I wrote.

The pale, spring-like green of my new jacket pleased me, and I was happy again.

"Sometimes a worm will sew a stitch in a young leaf, and even though the leaf may partly unfold, and partly grow and live, it will always be a crumpled and imperfect leaf . . . ," writes

Katharine Butler Hathaway. "Because the worm had sewed a stitch in me and made me forever crumpled, I belonged to the fantastic company of the queer, the maimed, the unfit."

I learned on the *Today Show* that actress Valerie Harper's new book was called *Today I Am a Ma'am*, and it was about growing older.

My feet were okay, but my right knee had been bothering me again, who knows why.

I preferred having an easy job that I could do perfectly, rather than a hard job that I couldn't, because I hated making mistakes.

The geometric pattern in my tin ceiling suddenly looked like gritted teeth.

"It's more suave to have no regrets," I wrote, "but I do have them."

It occurred to me that more boys should take off their shirts in the park.

I had to squeeze through a crowd to reach Psychology, because Valerie Harper was doing a book signing.

See *The Emotional Brain*, by Joseph LeDoux, page 12.

At the top of the subway steps, the blossoming trees were palest green against a pale, green-gray sky.

"I let my socks not matching go too far," said John as he cleaned his apartment, "and now I can't make heads or tails of them."

Ringing in my ears, probably from the Wellbutrin.

My friend David sent me a linocut he made of the Loch Ness Monster.

I began reading a book on the history of Latin America, in vignettes.

My arthritis doctor said, "If you think rheumatology is hit or miss, psychopharmacology is like when I was a little girl and I'd shut my eyes and point to which stuffed animal I wanted to sleep with that night."

In the dream I was listening to a Fifth Dimension sort of song that went:

> *Shagga dagga diddly—*
> *Shagga dagga diddly—*
> *Doo!*

I dreamed Martha Stewart guest-starred on *Love Boat*.

The plot was simple: Martha turned out not to be so uptight after all.

At the end of the show, Martha jumped in the pool with all her clothes on.

Down my street the horizon was bright yellow, and the blanket of clouds was soft, yellow and mauve, like a golden cloth with a purple sheen, and soon the pink part began.

It took all morning, but I didn't have to pay a fine for trespassing.

On the phone my friend Erin said, "I just got a bill from AT&T for forty-six cents, and they're not even my long distance carrier."

"He walks slowly, listening alertly because lost souls weep or sometimes whistle like the breeze," writes Eduardo Galeano. "When he finds the missing soul, the wizard-priest lifts it with the tip of a feather, wraps it in a tiny ball of cotton, and carries it in a little hollow reed back to its owner, who will not die."

I dreamed I was cutting up the American flag into confetti, and even now I can feel the cool scissors in my hand, the sensation of the thick cloth giving way, and the pleasure of it.

Journal: "Weird how rough a winter I had."

Journal: "When I lost a baby tooth, Mom had me drop it into a glass of water. I watched the hard little white thing float down to the bottom, and then we placed the glass on the shelf beside my bed. In the morning my tooth was gone, and a dime was in its place. It wasn't exactly a miracle but it was straightforward and predictable, and it helped mark my progress forward on the earth. This memory, though brief, gives me a warm, happy feeling."

I dreamed I was eating ferns.

HUMMINGBIRD

1

THE CRYING CHILD raised her two hands to her mother, asking to be lifted from the stroller, and to my surprise the mother in her wine-red sari did unbuckle her daughter and hoisted her up into her arms, the child's dress wine-red too, and when the mother turned away from me I could see the child's little face against her shoulder, utterly calmed and relieved.

On the lawns of Central Park the old trees presided over huge patches of deep shade.

In the gray street an old speckled gray dog, so fat as to be nearly spherical, had just produced four nearly spherical gray turds.

The difficulty of being honest or objective about your own life for more than a second.

The neurologist, Dr. Neophytides, shocked me with electrodes and stuck me with pins. Lying on my stomach I said, "It's too bad you can't do acupuncture at the same time." "Ha-ha!" he barked, ready to stick me again. "I give you as many as you want!"

Wellbutrin made my ears ring, so I switched to an older drug called nortriptyline, and the ringing seemed to grow slightly more faint but didn't entirely cease.

At the intersection of Atlantic Avenue and Vanderbilt, a pleasant, ocean-y smell.

It was July 2001 and I was reading D. H. Lawrence.

I had no neuropathy and only mild carpal tunnel syndrome, and Dr. Neophytides added with smiling, Old World confidence that the Neurontin he prescribed would certainly help my arthritis pain.

I climbed on top of John and he came, but then I couldn't come, which left me guilty and confused.

Back in California, my mother fell and cracked two ribs.

Obscuring the sunset was a huge blobby gray cloud, framed by dull-orange below and brilliant white-gold above, as if the cloud itself were the source of light.

I told John I had fantasized about the hot Hispanic guy we'd seen in the video store, and John said, "Olé!"

I asked if he, too, ever thought about someone else. "Sometimes," he said, diplomatically.

The large white poodle that refused to be pulled forward looked like Carol Channing.

On the E train, the sight of perfection in a tight T-shirt also left me guilty and confused.

The Neurontin worked every bit as well as Dr. N. said it would, and the first day I took it I also got in one of those moods where suddenly anything seems possible, so as I bicycled along the East River in Queens, I observed how the late afternoon sun poured straight down each avenue at this particular time of year, and I made plans to live and work in France.

I lost my temper and swore at the manager of the discount clothing store.

That spring I had received a small writing grant that enabled me to pay off all my debts, but now I was more than ready for something else nice to happen.

Nortriptyline was the last antidepressant invented before Prozac, and I like to think it could have been a hit if Prozac hadn't overshadowed it.

My job at the magazine is best described as putting on a tiger suit and jumping up and down in front of the bleachers all day.

Journal: "Lawrence's urge to coin hyphenated words, e.g. 'woman-presence,' is noble-misguided."

The rain poured from the dirty-chartreuse sky.

At the memorial gathering the editor-in-chief spoke fondly of the late chairman's ability to secure preferential treatment for top employees, such as "that hospital room that wasn't available" or help from the Immigration and Naturalization Service in obtaining citizenship.

It wasn't that I expected life to be fair, or rich people not to call in favors, but I was a little surprised that, far from questioning power, journalists would so brazenly seek to benefit from it.

Blanching, hazy light down Sixth Avenue, dark, edgeless clouds above, and flickers of lightning at the end of 34th Street, over the river.

I couldn't sleep because I was afraid there might be a mistake in my newsletter tribute to the late chairman.

The way the mind alights on one thing, and then another.

I let my hair grow and took to flipping it out of my eyes the way I had when I was, say, thirteen.

I was trying to cut down how often I went on the Internet to peer at photos of naked, muscular men.

The huge trees in full leaf began to look tired of their own magnificence, and it was August.

Since starting on antidepressants, I found that my various problems no longer seemed overwhelming but neither had they yielded solutions.

In the store full of nineteen-year-olds my friend Robert said, "I have a new saying: 'Babyhood is lost on the babies.'"

Later, as it continued raining, the sky was gray-orange with metal-green lightning cracks.

My problems continued to be whether and how John and I would ever live together, and whether and how I could find a better way to support myself.

I looked up Nortriptyline on the Internet to see if it, too, might be making my ears ring, though the more likely culprits were my various arthritis medicines, which I couldn't give up.

I lay there listening to Joni Mitchell and imagining I had been unjustly fired.

My friend Erin and I recalled the indignities of high school, and I said, "People are always talking about the problem of runaway teens. But the real question is, why aren't there *more*?"

2

"COME ON, COME on, hurry up!" I muttered to my penis, as it tried to pee.

How much of each day feels like blind thrashing.

A slot had opened up at the retirement home, so my parents were planning to move November 1, and I would have to go out to California in October to help them.

Of the four remaining siblings, I had the most flexible schedule, due to the magazine's generous vacation policy.

"I was so engrossed in MY stuff I didn't ask you where you went for the weekend and if you had a good time!! So tell me. Love, Mom."

I almost never dream about sex, and when I do it's almost always illicit sex.

I lay my head against his forbidden, muscled, Islamic belly, then kissed it, my boldness surprising me, because kissing it was even more forbidden.

My parents couldn't sleep because they were so worried about moving.

Despite the Nortriptyline I continued to tumble into very black moods from time to time, or more accurately, gray humors, vomit-green tantrums, and shit-brown funks, which left me hopeless, annoyed, and ashamed, respectively.

I joked to myself that if someone at work asked, "How are you?" I'd answer, "My daughter died."

John and I rolled over and went to sleep, but the next morning sex clicked in a way it hadn't in a while, and then we went bicycling.

Way out in the Rockaways, ugly red-brick housing projects, the A train a series of concrete archways like an aqueduct, and huge empty lots, whole tracts of land that you never see in New York anymore, then the old wooden boardwalk and the sea in little verdigris waves calmly rippling in.

Jean Rhys: "Yes, that night was the last frenzied effort of my guardian angel, poor creature."

3

A SHRIEK FROM my coworker who had a TV in her office.

And to think that only two days before, John and I had remarked how we could see the World Trade Center from the Rockaways.

Van Gogh: "We live in such a disturbed time that there can be no way of having opinions fixed enough to form any judgment of things . . . I have a landscape with olive trees and also a new study of a starry sky . . . When you have looked at these two studies for some time, it will perhaps give you some idea, better than words could, of the things that Gauguin and Bermard and I sometimes used to talk about."

Again and again, from various angles, the plane slicing into the tower.

With unusual kindness people moved aside to let me off the crowded subway car.

Noelle also saw clients in an office down near Wall Street, so I was terrified something might have happened to her, but fortunately she was fine.

The woman in the office next to mine shut her door because her cousin, a fireman, had been killed.

A mass e-mail from a new person in Marketing, asking for help in locating her brother.

Erin's three-week-old nephew suffocated in his crib in Maryland.

Each day Erin had to clean up the thin layer of ash that blew from Lower Manhattan into her windows in Brooklyn Heights.

"And now," said the cassette Noelle had given me, "begin relaxing, or maintain and enhance your relaxation, by focusing on breathing deeply, and slowly."

Erin asked me to read what she'd written to say at her nephew's funeral. In it, she affirmed the evolution of the soul.

Later, as we turned to leave the bar, I saw sitting next to me a middle-aged man with his eyes closed, perhaps in fatigue or meditation, which anyone right now was entitled to, I thought, but then I recognized him as an editor from the magazine where I worked, evidently pretending not to see me.

My parents decided not to move November 1 but to take the next opening at the retirement home, which could be several months away.

"Dad refuses to throw anything out."

I looked down and noticed someone had dropped a paper clip in the urinal.

John and I got into an argument over whether or not the suicide hijackers were "evil."

Rain falling on the disaster site made the whole city smell like burnt plastic, and downtown on the street corners and alongside the buildings, candles burned below photos of the missing.

I cried in front of the television because the President said absolutely nothing but they all stood and applauded anyway.

Rhys: "The country stretched flatly into an infinite and melancholy distance, but it looked to me sunlit and full of promise, like the setting of a fairy tale."

I delayed but did not cancel my trip to San Jose, because my parents still needed help cleaning out the house, even if they weren't moving immediately.

John and I watched *Creature from the Black Lagoon.*

At the Brooklyn Botanical Garden, near the greenhouses, a four-year-old prancing sideways: "Mom, is this walking?"

The *Times* printed my friend Cathy's letter asking "What is victory?" and subsequently she received hate mail.

Erin wasn't allowed to share her beliefs about reincarnation at her nephew's memorial service.

When the bus rumbled past, the angry pothole spewed water and black-tar pebbles across the entire sidewalk, but fortunately it missed me.

Useless fact: the discount store where I yelled at the manager was right across the street from the World Trade Center.

John's strategy was to read the *Times* thoroughly, while I found I could barely read it at all.

The magazine where I worked printed George W. Bush's inanities in huge letters below full-page photos of the disaster.

ABC said the Miss America Pageant would proceed tonight as planned and couldn't be stopped by terrorism.

Sad, tiny boy on the subway shaking off what his mom had just said to him.

4

THE THREE SECURITY men coming down the airplane's aisle said something about a passenger name matching one on their list of terrorists—but the passenger turned out to be a baby.

5

IN CUPERTINO HARDWARE I smelled alcohol on the breath of the man who mixed our paint.

Carried on the fragrant air, the screams of recess at my old grade school.

High up on the ladder I painted under the eaves, while my father watched.

A certain kind of moaning guitar solo reminds me more than anything else could of the hormone-soaked panic of my early teen years—the darkened rec rooms, the couples making out, the dope I was afraid to try.

My father didn't want to move to a retirement home, but my mother did.

His vision might not have declined so rapidly if his doctor had caught the problem sooner.

"What color do you call your hair?" he asked me. "Light brown?"

All over the yard my father had stockpiled dozens of plastic bleach containers filled with water, in case of an earthquake.

"John saw both towers collapse, from Fifth Avenue," I said over lunch.

I napped with a kind of exhaustion that might be called traumatized.

Since my parents weren't especially good at sympathy, I didn't expect anything special from them regarding 9/11, whose effect on me I couldn't quite grasp anyway.

Up on the ladder again, my gaze sometimes drifted from the creamy off-white eaves to the extraordinarily blue sky.

Mom's eyes had looked very red and irritated at lunch and I wondered if I should have been more forceful in suggesting she call the glaucoma doctor again.

By now it had dawned on me that not just this one part, but the entire house, badly needed painting.

Mom's hearing had gotten so bad that she couldn't play the violin anymore.

The tomatoes in the salad had to be peeled and cut into very little pieces, or my father couldn't chew them.

I supposed it was possible to feel traumatized by something that didn't affect you directly.

"You are a first-class idiot," I imagined telling my parents' doctor.

The lettuce, too, had to be torn into very little pieces.

Though it was only a part of the city that was destroyed, and not even my favorite part, still it's my city, and in this sense I did feel directly affected.

For years now the three of us had all kept our political views to ourselves, though this left fewer things to talk about.

"Mom knows how to cook anything," said Dad, as she poked at the just microwaved fish.

"Sit down and loaf, that's an order," he said to her after dinner.

On the cop show it eventually came out that the evil (fat) psychotherapist had implanted false memories of sexual abuse in the vulnerable mind of a young female patient.

"Okay, good night," I said, but they were both asleep in their chairs.

Either the Nortriptyline or the Neurontin made me see weird patterns if I woke up in the middle of the night—geometric bursts, flickering line segments, wiggly blobs.

6

A LARGE RED rubber band held the package of fake breakfast sausage closed.

Mom seemed much older than she had, say, a year before— more stooped, more frail—and Dad's vision was much worse.

"Do you think you'll want these at Sunny View?" I asked, and the two of them stood blinking at the folding lawn chairs, which were hanging on nails beside the Thunderbird, but they couldn't decide.

Huge softball fist of white-yellow magnolia between the huge waxy leaves of the tree across the street.

"See all that dirt?" Mom said, proudly holding up the bottom of the Swiffer for me to see.

Sometimes I'd get mixed up as to who could hear and who could see, particularly because my mother pretended to hear what she didn't, and my father pretended to see better than he did.

I laughed when Dad joked that maybe the ugly mustard-yellow house on the next street over was occupied by terror-ists, though I doubted he intended a broader point about right wing paranoia.

On the perfect, balmy breeze, a marching band playing "Louie Louie."

As Dad followed behind, I gathered up all the plastic bleach containers lying by the fence and alongside the house, poured out the water in each, and placed them in the yellow recycling bins. "There," I said.

In the old television cabinet, from which the picture tube had been removed, were a dozen or so old Tide boxes.

As I carried the leaky garden hoses to the trashcan, Dad said, "That's enough for today."

At lunch we discussed the recycling laws, which were complex, and the cracked driveway, which the house inspector had said would have to be repoured at a cost of $5,000.

Defiantly my father said he wouldn't do it, nor would he have the hot water heater raised eighteen inches off the garage floor.

"Her name sounds Italian but actually it's Indian," said Mom of the real estate agent. I looked again at the little picture on the pad of paper and saw that her features were indeed East Indian.

After lunch I napped the nap of the righteous.

We had moved to this house when I was ten, and on the wastebasket in my old room, Charlie Brown still said, "Good grief!"

In one of the *Britannica* Books of the Year—1968, I think—there was a picture of a Soviet gymnast that I used to copy in pencil, and that was how I taught myself to draw.

Bad arthritis in my hand from all that painting.

"I don't know what you're going to do when I'm not around anymore," Mom said playfully.
　　"I'll be sunk," Dad answered.
　　"I won't be here forever," she said, sounding almost relieved.
　　"I'll be sunk," Dad repeated.
　　I continued clearing the dinner table.
　　"I guess you'll have to marry Hattie B.," Mom said to him.
　　He chuckled. "Yes, I'll have to marry Hattie B."
　　"Who's Hattie B.?" I asked, from the sink.

"Just someone from church," Mom said. "She's a very nice person, *but*."

I laughed. "You mean she's unattractive?"

"No, actually she has a very nice figure," said Dad. "But she gets very upset if things don't go the way she thinks they should at church."

"Is it Hattie, or Pattie?" I asked.

"Hattie," said Dad. He came over to dry the dishes. "And her husband's name was Bee, B-E-E. Hattie Bee."

"Hattie Bee," I repeated.

I went through the Christmas things, saving the best ornaments and the giant old lights to mail to myself, because I knew John would love them.

The Christmas box was so old that its promotional message read, "Special Price: 7¢ off."

7

Dad spilled water on the counter and Mom whispered, "This is what I have to deal with all the time."

The last time I'd seen Noelle, which was before the attacks, she had explained the Oedipal Complex in a way that felt new and revelatory.

I couldn't remember now what she had said, only that it was indeed complex.

In the local newspaper Anna Deavere Smith wrote that the fires of the World Trade Center smelled "like a dragon, yawning"—as if the event needed embellishment.

Sometimes Mom said "Excuse me" after complaining about my father, because she knew I didn't like it.

My father kept a dozen suits in his study closet, going back to 1980, he said, and on each lapel was pinned a small slip of paper with the waist size (38½, now too small), which he asked me to read for him.

"I don't like to give anything away," he said, sliding the closet door closed again.

As I dragged the old eight-track stereo from under his workbench, he said, "This is going too fast for me," something he had said before, but this time I understood the obvious, that he wasn't ready to move.

"I *ask* him and *ask* him to throw things away!" Mom whispered in the kitchen.

"I don't think you get much for your money in a retirement home," said Dad in the side yard.

"He just doesn't *concentrate*," said Mom in her study.

I walked the deserted, heat-drenched streets trying to calm myself down.

Above my old schoolyard, the dry, pink mountains of yore.

At dinner Mom said, "When you were nine or ten you came home from Roger's—his parents were divorced—and you said, 'You and Dad aren't getting a divorce, are you?'"

"HERE ARE KEN'S papers," said Mom, meaning the diary my brother Ken had kept during the last five years of his life. "I tried reading it, but it was too painful. I didn't know he was in so much pain, that he was so depressed."

She handed me the sealed manila envelope.

Often I wasn't able to respond meaningfully when my parents told me emotionally charged things, such as the above.

I had long known of the existence of the diary Ken had kept before he died of AIDS, and I was glad that it existed, but even then, twelve years after his death, I was afraid to read it.

Above my old bed were the copper-colored brackets and redwood-stained shelves I had put up as a teenager, as well as my quaint nature photographs—columbine in shady forest; orchard in springtime.

I had once hid a cummy sheet under my bed, and when I looked again it was covered with tiny black ants.

I thanked God that tomorrow I was going away for a couple of days, to visit friends.

". . . and thank you for Cliff's help," said Mom during grace.

While Dad dozed in his chair, she and I watched a documentary about New York City, whose aerial shots of the twin towers made my eyes well up.

"I know, it's freaky, it's just really freaky," I said to my sister Carol, who had called from France.

"I observed certain things that indicated that the house was slipping forward," said the e-mail from my other sister, Helen, regarding a dream that combined her own town-house, my parent's house, and the World Trade Center. "Then you-all pulled up in the car, sort of down the hill from the house (which was on a hill), and I yelled down for you to stay away and get away fast, as the house was slipping; I ran down the hill, and then the house suddenly slipped very fast, but instead of sliding forward it slid backwards and sort of collapsed as it disappeared over the hill."

I regret that my continuing anger at my mother, over her complaining about my father, often kept me from her.

I noted the fragrance of the lemon tree overhanging the fence, and Dad said, "Delightful."

Mom pulled back the drape to point out to me the full moon.

When she said, "I'm not going to be here forever," I saw how she truly believed it—that is, that she would continue to exist, just not *here*—and for a brief moment this seemed not simply a matter of loss for me but an objective fact for each of us.

Again and again those shots of smoldering piles of steel and rubble, and rescue workers still holding out hope for survivors.

"I'm glad we were able to do it," said Mom of caring for Ken during his two major illnesses.
"Our poor little Ken," said Dad.

9

ALWAYS INTERESTING TO take the train in California, because no one does.

At the station coffee shop, a mom said to her six-year-old, "You're always going to be my son, no matter what."

"To disseminate anthrax germs with a crop duster," the *Times* cheerfully explained, "terrorists would have to master dozens of complex steps."

This particular train passed through many beautiful, swampy places.

Red and green succulents along the levees, and the gray bay stretching away flatly below the even gray sky.

Tender, burned-seeming buttocks of a grass-shaved hill.

Sometimes I did actually pray when Mom said grace, as tainted as organized religion is for me.

John doesn't believe in the afterlife, but I do.

There was a very smart girl I knew from church, probably a dyke, who left home and got her own apartment at sixteen (was she abused?); for a time she and I worked in the same nursing home, as dishwashers; a few years later I heard she had become addicted to glue.

Memories don't have to be relevant to be meaningful.

A bird with a very long beak flew down from a telephone wire.

10

OVER DINNER WITH Cathy I discussed my father's failing vision, my mother's diminishing hearing, my father's patchy memory, my mother's osteoporosis, asthma, allergies, as well as their feelings about each of these things, and my feelings, my denial.

11

"BOTH MY PARENTS are gentle, lovely people," I told my friend Gabby, "despite their many problems."

Whenever I stayed with Gabby I got to sleep in the cabin in her backyard, which was almost like camping.

When I was five my father worked in another state for about six months, and I recall not quite recognizing him as he made popcorn in the kitchen one evening—a painful memory I've never been able to understand in any useful way.

I thought, "Who is that nice man making popcorn?"

That was in Illinois; hollyhocks grew in the side yard.

At the end of the block, a park with tall trees—some fallen with the roots exposed.

Mom forbade me to dress up in her old clothes again, and

then she asked why I only played with my friend Liz and not the other little boys on the block—a question I had never even considered and therefore couldn't begin to answer.

I hope that simple, factual sentences about my childhood will make the past seem almost comprehensible—not "normal" exactly, but closer to it—that is, an objective story I can view without shame.

Superman was a turn-on.

The basement used to flood regularly.

The pipes froze.

Though the reasons for my father's absence in 1963 were always explained as purely practical—we had to remain in Wheaton until the house was sold, and the house was difficult to sell—I gather that, for various reasons including the house itself, my parents were very much at odds during this period.

Family story: My older brother Ken said, "If you don't like it, you can lump it," and I said, "Lump lump lump—I lumped it!"

Liz showed me how to pick wild strawberries in the empty lot next door.

I liked the retired couple in the house on the other side of ours but Mom told me not to bother them.

Before he got the job in New Orleans, my father had been unemployed off and on for nearly a year, and my mother had been very worried about money.

She had to go to work as a Kelly Girl to pay my sisters' college tuition.

She herself had attended only junior college. The day before she was supposed to leave for Grinnell, her father's salary was cut in half and she couldn't go. She cried all night.

Jack LaLanne: also a turn-on.

"Little Cliff, little Cliff, little Cliff-Cliff-Cliff," my father used to say.

At nursery school I was sent to naptime early because I called Liz a "nincompoop."

Liz got off by maintaining she had only called me a "nincom."

The vibration of Mom's voice as she held me in her arms.

I had hidden behind the big beige chair in the living room, and when Ken found me, he kept saying, "Where are you? Where are you? You're invisible!" until I screamed for him to make me appear again.

There was no bathroom in Gabby's cabin, and entering the house would wake her, so usually I just peed somewhere in the yard.

Quite pleasurable as well to imagine I *was* Superman.

12

"I WON'T ARGUE with you," said Mom to a cement truck merging in front of her on the freeway.

"He might pour concrete on you," said my father, who could no longer drive.

"Maybe he'll follow us home to our cracked driveway."

Using a sharp knife my father cut his chocolate cream into thin slices.

"I called them and told them that that magazine was for my *great-granddaughter*, not for my husband," my mother said. "I told them, 'My husband is eighty-eight and I'm eighty-six. What would we want with a *teen* magazine?'"

"I've sunken into myself," she said, later. "I don't have a waist anymore."

A sore throat told me I'd caught Gabby's cold.

"We didn't know where our next dollar was coming from," Mom said, referring to the period in Illinois when Dad was out of work.

Not feeling well, I napped the rest of the afternoon.

During *Antiques Roadshow* Mom reminded me that my great-grandfather on her side had been orphaned by an Indian attack in Kansas.

"Do you want to see our antiques?" my father asked, and he

returned with a wooden dough-mixing trough, two magnifying glasses, a handsome pair of cast-iron tailor's shears, and a small wooden device that he thought had something to do with spinning.

He reminded me that tomorrow I had to help him inspect the roof repairs made that week, since he couldn't see well enough to judge.

Mom made a face when Dad forgot to turn up the sound after a commercial.

I realized I didn't care how Detective Olivia would solve the crime, so I went to my room to jack off and go to sleep.

13

DAD PORED OVER the TV guide with one of the antique magnifying glasses.

"Do you want slossage?" Mom asked, using her playful word for sausage.

Each day the local newspaper breathlessly reported utterly useless information on terrorism leaked by "senior government officials."

My father and I on the roof.

I didn't think it had been fixed properly, but Dad said, "It looks much better," so I let it go.

(Nap.)

At the other end of the house Mom was crossly pointing out something that Dad had misunderstood, and he said, "I guess I'm just a dumb jerk then."

Dad was such an asshole when I was a teenager that I forgot I loved him and only began to remember after Ken died.

His virulent racism. His rants against taxes and foreign aid. His intolerance of any other view.

If I left a wrinkle in the bathroom rug, he would call to me, in a mock-mincing voice, "Oh, *Clifford*, come in here and tidy the rug."

He went now to the kitchen for a spoon with which to eat the chocolate chip cookie crumbs left in the canister.

Soon enough it was time to pick up my sister Helen at the airport.

My mother and father each hugged her, and then I got to hug her too.

To Helen Dad repeated his favorite stories: the division he worked for was shut down a year or two after he retired, because no one could do his job as well as he did; they had said he was too young to retire, and they had asked him to stay, but he had retired anyway; later they asked him to come back, but he refused, because he was enjoying retirement too much.

Later I overheard Dad tell Helen he could see well enough to drive if he wanted to, which wasn't true.

In the garage I stood looking up at the many empty boxes, trying to pick one that would be about the right size.

Dad gave me Ken's Mexican leather jewelry box, whose contents included four fortune cookie slips:
"An affectionate message, good tidings will come shortly."
"You will be asked to a wedding soon."
"You will overcome obstacles to achieve success."
"Success in everything."

Joan Didion once complained that a particular detail regarding a murder made for too obvious an irony, but she noted it anyway.

To my surprise, my brother Ken's old girlfriend, from before he was gay, e-mailed me. I hadn't spoken to her since the memorial service, in 1989.

While Dad and Helen napped, I tried to listen as Mom talked about their HMO, because health care was important, but afterwards I felt complicit with the accompanying complaints about my father.

A new cosmos: in the rafters of my parents' garage was an infinite number of cardboard boxes, left over from an infinite number of Christmases, birthdays, and anniversaries, and within each was an infinite number of boxes, and so on.

Helen and I knelt in Mom's study wrapping Christmas ornaments in tissue paper for mailing.

At the top of the box we placed the thick envelope that said "FOR CLIFF/RE: KEN."

We didn't learn of the air strikes on Afghanistan until my oldest brother, Paul, called from Boston to say hello.

Christine's e-mail told of how she had fallen out of touch with Ken and hadn't even known he was sick when she received the call inviting her to his memorial service.

Every story is simultaneously being written from someone else's point of view.

After I replied to Christine's e-mail she was anxious to speak to me, and though I had told her I was in San Jose that week, she tried to call me in Brooklyn and then e-mailed me that she hadn't been able to reach me.

"My vision is really bad," my father lamented.
    "Is it like you're wearing sunglasses all the time?" I asked.
    "No, it's like there's a cloudy film over my eyes."

Helen and I selected expensive peaches in the fancy supermarket. I didn't mention to her that Christine had contacted me, nor did I tell my parents, because it just seemed too complicated a subject for my last day in San Jose.

Sublime and stately, the huge old magnolia in the calmly dying light.

Mom's stories: the uncooked broccoli on the cruise ship; the uncooked potato, the rude waiter, and the inedible rice pudding on a different cruise ship; Mom locked out of the house by Dad; Mom locked out of the house by my sister Carol when she was two; the riverboat that had to go to Cincinnati because the river was too high to go to St. Paul; the pretentious woman in the tour group who mistakenly cracked her soft-boiled egg into her tiny egg cup; the first time Paul saw a "colored person," whom he called a "dirty man"; Dad spilling his water in a dark restaurant and not noticing, which made Ken and Mom laugh; Mom and my late aunt laughing at the dinner table, when they were kids, because they could see the sun shining through their Uncle Al's huge ears.

At breakfast Helen said she disagreed with the bombing, that it would only make things worse, and with some of the old ferocity my father said we had to strike back or they'd just do it again.

As I packed, Mom and Dad argued in the kitchen over whether Dad could see well enough to drive me to the airport. Fortunately Mom won.

Mom patted my shoulder and smiled as I sat down to breakfast.

In the car Dad said, "We will miss you."

At the airport gate a stewardess walked by and sat with the other stewardesses but said nothing to them, not even hello, and I thought, "What if you're a stewardess and the other stewardesses don't like you?"

14

OF MY BROTHER'S homosexuality, Christine said, "I think it was a phase, and he got stuck in it." As far as I knew, Ken had slept only with men for the last eight years of his life. Moreover, he had told me unequivocally that he was gay. "Huh—really?" I asked. "Ken went through phases," Christine replied. "He did everything in extremes." This was an interesting and possibly true statement, which I would have liked to evaluate apart from her views on his sexuality. She said there had been a period when he dropped acid twice a week and went surfing both morning and night, and in college they had had sex two or three times a day. "Our friends called us the rabbits," she said. I had known this to be their mutual endearment but had never known why. "You have to understand," she declared, "Ken was *not* like other people." In Christine's telling he began to take on a scary-alluring aura not unlike the scary-alluring aura that drugs, surfing, and sex had held for me when I was thirteen and looked up to my presumably straight brother who was in college. Christine's stories: All their friends would come over at two every day to get high and watch *Highway Patrol*, and they used to have nude swimming parties in the apartment complex pool. Throwing trash out the car window at Jack in the Box, Ken said, very stoned, "I'm contributing to the gross national product!" In his living room he apologized to a potential roommate for the mess, offered him a beer, then realized there was a cigarette floating in the bottle—"Oh, I guess you don't want that," Ken said. After my father refused to pay for graduate school in math, Ken tried to work his way through, flunked out his first semester, and grew dangerously depressed. Strolling on the beach one evening, on acid, Ken said, "Why don't we go walk along the moonbeam?" Sometimes he used to risk surfing between the pilings of the pier, at night. He asked Christine if she wanted to do a three-way, and she said no. In the Sierras he tried skiing down the most difficult slope and wiped out spectacularly. Later, after he and Christine had broken up and he had begun sleeping with men, he scandalized his old college friends by arriving at a party in white satin shorts. So much new information, from so long ago, confused me, and my brother's image grew unsteady in my mind. I wished I hadn't called Christine so late, my first night back in Brook-lyn. I remembered once finding in Ken's desk drawer, not long after he came out to me—this would have been about 1979—a slip of paper on which he had written over and over the name Keith Cody—same initials as Ken Chase. Had he ever used the name with a trick? Maybe Christine was right: my brother was a chameleon, simply trying on different iden-tities to see how each of them felt. Maybe he never knew who he was. "Two or three years after we broke up," she was telling me now, "he called me, out of the blue, and asked me to marry him." She saw this as proof that Ken was never really gay. "I said no," she continued, explaining that she had already met her current husband. I wondered why, in that case, she ob-jected so much to the idea that Ken was gay, since apparently she didn't want him anyway. The conversation exhausted me—constantly sifting everything Christine said, trying to de-cide what was true and to what degree. And conversely won-dering what were my own myths about my brother, what had I never understood about him? "I'm beginning to see that Ken was more bisexual than I thought," I offered. She replied, "He was tri-sexual—he'd try anything." I didn't know what to say to this joke, which seemed decades old. At some point I men-tioned that Ken had joined Narcotics Anonymous two years before he died, to quit his pot habit, and Christine replied, "Naturally he would throw himself into that role, too." I hadn't intended to bolster her phases theory. "I guess he really was self-medicating with the pot," I ventured. "For depres-sion, I mean. That was one of the hardest things for me to deal with after he died—that he wasn't a very happy man." "Oh, he was happy," Christine said quickly. "Back in college. He was very happy then." Evidently she meant to reassure me, but I could hardly feel reassured by the idea that my brother's life had been downhill from age twenty-two until his death at thirty-seven. I wanted to get off the phone now. I had always liked Christine and even looked up to her as a corollary to looking up to my brother. And I had felt enormous sympathy for her when she told me, at the beginning of the conversation, that her father had died suddenly, in a car accident, only a month before Ken—whose death, from her point of view, was also sudden, since she hadn't known of his illness. I had imagined moreover that the particular pain of losing her ex-lover would have been difficult to explain to those around her, since by then she was married with a young daughter. So I had hoped our interaction that night would be helpful to both of us, but apparently we were at cross-purposes. I said good-night, pleading jet lag. Then I couldn't sleep.

15

ON THE CROWDED platform a boy pretended to drop coins: "Clink. Clink-clink-clink," he said.

The continued glacially slow unfolding of non-news on TV.

Noelle said, "The collapse of the World Trade Center has so much symbolic meaning I can't even begin to fathom it."

"Calm down," I told myself, as I entered the fray of Bed Bath & Beyond.

A friend told me about a video artist who slowed down the movie *Psycho*, so that it lasts twenty-four hours.

Of Christine, Gabby wrote, "I think *she's* stuck."

I joked to John that an American flag on the antenna of a police car was gilding the lily.

I returned from the bathroom and found myself suddenly in the mood—it had been weeks.

John's incredibly delicate, sustained touch . . .

As he read the paper I asked him for the butter, and he replied, with mock annoyance, "Excuse me, I'm busy trying not to get *blown up.*"

E-mail from my mother: ". . . Sorry to 'dump' on you but I needed to blow off steam."

One of the columnists at the magazine where I worked suggested it was time we "consider" torturing suspected terrorists.

I imagined changing my out-of-office e-mail reply to "Eat me."

Soon it was the weekend again and John and I saw the most incredible gingko tree, huge and bright yellow in the light.

We descended toward the river, which was now pea green.

Charles Henri Ford: "To understand the mystery of our being in time—the body's reason and the soul's future—enough for a lifetime's meditation, without bothering about the stars, space and infinity."

As seen from the promenade, the water was evenly gray and shining under the clouds, and the breeze seemed to be licking it clean.

I suddenly realized it had been naïve of me to think Christine could be objective about my brother—her ex-lover, after all, who had left her to be gay—and it didn't matter how many years ago that was.

My parents' cruise was canceled because the Delta Queen Steamboat Company went bankrupt.

The box containing Ken's diary, which I had sent to myself at work, was held up in the mailroom for several days, because of an anthrax scare.

At the editors' meeting I attended, they smiled secretly to one another whenever a certain editor spoke, and they asked her questions as if she were a child.

I know that jockeying for position is simply human nature, a pack animal thing, but it has always revolted me.

We kept hearing the phrase "back to normal," and John said, "What if you didn't like normal?"

Down the platform, a low clarinet trilled.

The editors told me to submit the torture column for an award.

So I didn't know what Ken was on his way to before he died: so what?

Though the fire continued burning, the city seemed to have gotten used to the hole in the ground, and people in the news began arguing about how to rebuild, and what sort of memorial there should be.

I used the coupon Mom gave me to buy my own Swiffer.

It also occurred to me that Christine's father's death, coming so close to Ken's, must have completely overshadowed the latter event, preventing her from examining her feelings about my brother, and this might be why her perceptions of him seemed trapped in amber.

"I *can* be intimate," I told Noelle, getting back down to business, "I know how to do that, but then I seem to need to withdraw—why is that?"

"One bright thing in my life right now," wrote my mother, "is a hummingbird that has been coming to drink the nectar from the Bouganvilla (spelling?) that has been blooming profusely since I started watering it when I do the watering of the roses. This morning, it was there when a squirrel came running along on top of the fence and the bird flew up and hovered around as though it were saying, 'Squirrel, get out of here. I want my snack.' Then as soon as the squirrel left, down to a blossom came the bird. It is so wonderful to watch."

Over time Ken's image in my mind no longer seemed upsettingly changeable, as I gradually grew accustomed to the new information gleaned from Christine.

To a female passerby, a homeless man said, "You love me, I love you. It's very simple. Very simple indeed."

After a good cry my face looked rosy and healthy in the mirror.

"And now I'd like to watch *Star Trek* in peace," I muttered.

In the morning the editor-in-chief was happy to announce that the magazine didn't have anthrax after all, and soon enough the box from San Jose arrived in my office.

Mom was very worried they wouldn't get their $4,000 back from the trip insurance. "Dad never wanted to go on that trip in the first place."

I decided to try BuSpar, for anxiety, but it, too, made the tinnitus worse, so I had to stop.

Near the end of the dream, after witnessing a male rape, I received my map and instructions from my mother.

Outline for the previous few months: my usual problems; the suicide hijackings; my parents' mortality; my brother's life and death; my usual problems.

What a sight I must have been in the park, a man in a suit and tie stooping to collect fallen yellow leaves.

Ken was alive to me again for those few weeks following my conversation with Christine, in that he was still able to surprise me; just as I knew he would be alive to me again when I decided to read his diary.

John loved all the ornaments I'd sent from home.

"This film is a record of a journey," said *The New Yorker*, "and it leaves us with the dreadful possibility that all highways are lost."

I told Noelle, "I want a new fucking map, and new instructions."

Outside it was already dark. I walked up Lexington Avenue.

AM I GETTING WARMER?

1

UPPER QUAD WAS a clearing in the redwoods, lower quad a knoll overlooking the ocean; I lived in lower quad, in Dorm 8.

January 1980, my senior year: a prehistoric time, crucial but shrouded.

In this foray into the past, I consider previous quests for maps and instructions.

With some pride I put on my surplus khakis and the white button-down shirt I had discovered in a box at my parents' house over Christmas break—my new look.

That fall I had cut my hair for the first time since high school, and grown my first beard.

Between the two quads lay a courtyard and the dining hall, which also overlooked the ocean; by the steps was a white stucco wall covered in bougainvillea, which bloomed year-round.

As the brand-new record strummed its cockeyed beat, I

stared at the five of them on the cover: angular cut-outs on a flat, horizonless yellow—three boys, two girls—defiant in their thrift-shop clothes and poofy wigs.

Journal entry: "Legitimate (I think) fears and desires concerning my sexuality are taking the form of guilt."

Remembering that time requires extra kindness toward myself.

I spooned fuchsia-colored yogurt from the plastic tub.

Under a vaulted timber ceiling, I pulled the heavy blue *Canterbury Tales* from the shelf marked with the course number.

For now, let the white space between these sentences stand for what couldn't be seen then; or what can't be remembered now; or my open fate; or the open, bare-bones arrangement of a B-52's song (drum kit, guitar, cheesy keyboard, toy piano)—my soundtrack that winter and spring.

"The person who is writing this journal is perhaps on his way out," I wrote.

I walked toward some dark trees in the dry yellow light under a pale turquoise cloudless sky.

Particular tension of standing with my tray on the edge of the dining hall, deciding whom to sit with.

My friends: 1. Every night at about nine, Cathy came up to my room with the backgammon board and I pulled our favorite record from its bright yellow jacket. 2. Like me, Chris had sandy blond hair, a light brown beard, and glasses, and he covered his mouth and looked sideways when he laughed, as if, also like me, he dwelt perpetually in high school study hall. 3. E. (a girl)—peripheral then; central later—was "intensely neurotic," I wrote to a friend. 4. I've known Mike since I was twelve, so describing him is like describing the air.

"And also, now that Ken is gay," my journal continues, "I have lost one more person to identify with. I used to imitate him quite a bit, I think. But now that is impossible, unless I want to be gay."

Though I wrote "now that"—as if the event were recent— Ken had come out to me almost a year earlier.

The beeping at the start of "Planet Claire": signal from some distant part of myself.

Cathy's short, blond hair, thick glasses and slightly crossed brown eyes; her husky-fluty Peppermint Patty laughter.

I sat alone in the sunshine on last year's tall dry grass, below which new grass had sprouted with the rain and was already a few inches tall.

I made a pen and ink drawing of a cluster of trees.

Mike and I ran side by side down the rocky path—pleasure of my feet hitting the earth, in rhythm with his.

The campus was spread across hills and ravines of redwoods, bay trees, the occasional maple, live oaks, ferns, and vast stretches of tall waving grass—emerald in winter, golden the rest of the year.

In the professor's office I recited the opening of *The Canterbury Tales*, in Middle English, enjoying the odd-sounding yet familiar words on my tongue and in my throat.

We received narrative evaluations instead of grades (a grand 1960s experiment, later abandoned), and stringy-haired guys sold pot out of gigantic black garbage bags in their dorm rooms.

I was attending the stoner school of all time and I didn't even like pot.

When Chris encountered any sort of falseness or stupidity, he said "Ew" in a quick, guttural way that reminded me I had found a fellow traveler in disgust.

The year before, I had decided the people in the campus Christian group I belonged to were creeps, and I left the group.

I began saying "Ew" exactly as Chris did, and soon Cathy did, too.

I was in the process of forming myself, as if from nothing, from what was available—my classes, my records, my second-hand clothes, my new friends and our running jokes, my letters to and from old friends—as if from popsicle sticks, tin foil, and yarn.

To explain Middle English pronunciation to E., I recast a Michael Jackson song as "Ee lavah the way ye shakah yourrr thingah."

The closet as a kind of innocence.

In Chaucer I was learning to distinguish the teller and his limitations from the tale itself.

"The sturdy and flamboyant Wife of Bath finds herself at a transitional time of life," I wrote.

Though I wasn't a Christian anymore, I still believed viscerally in things like demon possession and the notion that certain actions inevitably bring punishment.

Piercing retro sci-fi organ of "There's a Moon in the Sky."

I have little memory of those evenings with Cathy, as if our study breaks took place beyond the long arm of self-consciousness.

My grandmother's crazy quilt beneath the backgammon board.

The click of dice and checkers, the crackle of the record player.

Cathy and I were barely more than acquaintances then and couldn't have known we were also knitting a lifelong friendship.

We never danced, instead playing quietly like good children, occasionally bouncing a foot to the quirky tunes.

Screechy guitar. Fred Schneider shouting, "HELLO?" We laughed. More screechy guitar. "HELLO?"

Outside my dorm room window—moonlight, redwoods, the open dry fields descending to the ocean.

In the cool morning air I crossed a ravine on the footbridge, shaded by tangled bay trees.

The Iranian hostage crisis was in full swing, but I didn't own a TV.

In the clothing store in Monterey, the clerk asked if I was in a fraternity, I said no, we didn't have fraternities at Santa Cruz, he seemed disappointed, I tried on a sport coat, he stood behind me grazing my butt with his fingers, explaining that that was exactly where the jacket should fall.

Slashing guitar sets up pleasure in my throat, a sensation identified by Wayne Koestenbaum with regard to the opera fan, but I think it applies to all musical enjoyment—a silent, sympathetic hum in the vocal cords.

"I'm afraid again tonight that there is so much keeping me from ever having a sexual relationship," I wrote in my journal. ". . . I keep allowing myself to . . . laugh at a certain moment, turn my head at a certain moment, etc.—to defuse sexuality."

Cathy liked to imitate the way the girls sang "Jackie O," the percussive *k*, the long *o*.

I tried to think about women when I masturbated and often succeeded.

"But the Wife of Bath has expressed earlier an almost despairing awareness of the intractability of her own spirit,

68

which is unwilling to restrain its 'immoral' impulses."

Were my professors perhaps moved by how lost I was?

The guy with washboard abs playing Ping-Pong; the hairy-chested guy riding his skateboard in and out of the quad; the poet-mathematician who lingered in my dorm room one night and I didn't know why; the guy who wore shorts all winter, who invited me into his dorm room, shut the door, and lay there grinning at me through his sparse but attractive beard, and I didn't know why.

"Dance this mess around."

The paved path skirted a dry, sunny hillside.

I'm trying to grasp the nature of dreaming and living despite myself.

Wet Speedo of a professor hanging to dry on the casement window of his office.

Periodically Cathy and I tried to parse this odd, ironic kind of music that was totally new to us—playful, nostalgic, assembled from junk and nonsense.

We misidentified the opening "Peter Gunn" riff as James Bond, though this correctly located the sound in childhood memories of sexiness, swank, and intrigue, as seen on TV.

We decided that the planet where people had no heads was San Jose, the endless suburb where Cathy, too, had grown up.

The one openly gay student I knew seemed to dwell on the outside of everything—I always saw him sitting alone in the same spot, on bare concrete, his back against the rough concrete wall, rolling a cigarette.

I lay in bed with a cold, my fourth that year.

Dream: "A vague sex scene of great passion. I am avoiding saying that I kissed his ass, and that it was extremely smooth and muscular and white . . . I was in a sense a different person—fear and conscience and guilt siphoned off. Except . . . I think my mother was there."

The year before, after the gay grad student moved out of the dorm, the stoners claimed to have found a jar of Vaseline under his bed.

I ran alone through the dry scrub and woods.

I stopped to say hi to a girl from the dorm named Patty. She said, "You look cute in your running shorts." "With these skinny arms?" I asked, lifting them. She shook her head. "It's the whole *package*, Cliff." I ran on.

These ideas about myself, in the forest of myself.

I hadn't even kissed a girl (or anyone) since I was 14.

In "There's a Moon in the Sky," Fred assured me that if I felt like a misfit, there were, in fact, "thousands of others like you! Others like you!" and since he didn't specify what those others were, I didn't have to be afraid.

Queer child looks up at the night sky, in search of sympathy.

"E. and I and Chris and another guy slept outside last Friday night," I wrote in my journal. "E. and I stayed up talking, and reality began to fade. She began to say how no one was ever attracted to her. So I (fearfully) said that I didn't consider our friendship as entirely Platonic . . . She said, 'Well, thanks. I think you're attractive too.' I felt brushed aside."

We woke surrounded by cows.

I wrote, "Perhaps I need to allow myself to be a fool, to fail, to cease analyzing, to get drunk, to make a pass . . . How does romance 'happen'?"

I arranged to have a picnic with Marya, a girl I knew from my dorm the previous year.

We lay on a blanket in a field and I was almost attracted to her—her white round face and long peasant skirt.

It's as if my own desire were a doll—I was always trying to make it do things, act out a story, sit or stand or pretend to walk.

Marya and I talked "deeply," there on the grass in the sun, but then we folded up the blanket and walked back to the dorms without even a kiss.

I wrote of *The Nun's Priest's Tale:* "The Priest also appears quite interested in the problem of 'vanitee,' in a broad sense of the word as inadequate and illusory ways of thinking (and speaking) that inevitably deceive and prejudice us . . ."

Fred Schneider's unsuccessful attempt to call a number written on the bathroom wall—"I dial stupid number ALL DAY LONG!"

Journal: "I had set a goal for myself to become sexually involved with someone before I graduate. I would have few regrets about UCSC if that happened . . ."

It seems like Cathy and I spent many months playing backgammon and listening to records, but actually it was only a single quarter, just ten weeks.

Motown fragments in "Dance This Mess Around": my introduction to pastiche.

"Ska-doo-da-bop—Eeww": delight or disgust?

The enigma of "Rock Lobster": my introduction to nonsense, and its importance.

Cathy graduated; I had one more term to go.

2

FOR AS LONG as I can remember, I have castigated myself for not properly enjoying things, first toys, later people, moments, and landscapes.

No record or memory of what I did over spring break.

Patch of pale blue ocean in the distance, which I always tried to appreciate as lovely and serene, but which mostly seemed to disappear in my mind.

The stoners sat shirtless in front of the dorm; constant snickering and hacking and mulling over "buds" and "sinsemilla"; continual drone of Pink Floyd, speakers pointed out the window.

I was indeed lost to myself and on myself and yet I was also completely myself, as much as any weird prehistoric creature was itself, if doomed, if purely transitional on the evolutionary ladder, completely itself and utterly unseen, except for the fossil, a kind of shadow across time.

Chris and I jumped over the four-foot wall that everyone jumped over to get to the mailboxes.

It was beautiful everywhere you looked: bright gold poppies appeared in all the fields, and wisteria draped the walkways of the college next to mine.

I sat on a bench in the sunshine reading my evaluations.

My Chaucer professor praised my "detailed familiarity with the text" as well as my "hard work and keen intelligence."

I enrolled in his course on Spenser's *Faerie Queene.*

The fiction teacher let me into her workshop because I said I liked Flannery O'Connor.

"Let the games begin," said Chris, imitating a creature on *Star Trek*, and he pretended to click his alien fingers. "Khee! Khee!"

Cathy came to visit for a few days, before moving to New York; she slept on the floor of my dorm room.

"I finally got up the nerve to ask her to sleep with me . . . I got scared though. We kissed and held each other. I was shaking. Eventually I relaxed though. We couldn't have intercourse because she had no protection . . . I never came . . . We laughed a lot and made jokes while we were making love . . . Finally we just went to sleep . . . I felt like I had gone as far as I wanted . . . such a shock, really, to make love, to be naked, to sleep with another . . . the night was awful. I couldn't sleep . . . I felt so boxed in with her sleeping beside me, in the narrow bed . . . In the morning we made love a bit more . . . She seemed to be doing the wrong thing. I just felt rubbed and wiggled . . . She would breath in my ear and lick it and I would practically go wild. But when she tried to make me come, I couldn't."

Fred yelling "having fun!"—either forced, manic enjoyment or enraged sarcasm.

Mike asked, "Well, Cliff, wasn't it pleasurable?"

I started seeing a counselor at the university's health center.

Now that Cathy was gone, I listened to the B-52's by myself.

Cindy or Kate going "wild" over her idol, growling, screeching—

At breakfast I overheard someone say the super muscular guy from Dorm Six had freaked out on acid, and it took several people to hold him down; I feigned disinterest, stirring my burned granola.

The cafeteria overlooked the distant bay, like a restaurant in a National Park.

I lay in bed with another bad cold, my fingers grazing the short, brown, napless carpet.

Dream: "Ken's arm was cut off. He was acting strangely, down and out . . . He said his supervisor pulled at his arm and it came off . . . [Later] Mom sent me a letter saying something like, 'I no longer curse fate. My rebellious children are mutilated, slain, ill . . .'"

I policed everything I thought and said but occasionally let slip a telling lie: of Mike's red-haired roommate, I said, "His hair is the most amazing color. What I want to know is, does he have a sister?"

Looking back at myself then is a little like watching *Mr. Magoo.*

Mike was tall, with dirty-blond hair that curled on his shoulders, gray eyes, a wide face and aquiline nose.

Regarding psychotherapy: "I feel so ugly, bleeding, exposed. And I need to be exposed. The rationalizations are fading . . . Greg [my therapist] said I have to come down from the mountain and be part of the human race . . . I feel so ugly, so juvenile, so wrong, wrong, wrong."

". . . letting go, losing control, being ugly, bloody, gaping, awkward, driven, limp-wristed, ineffectual, but whole, alive, washed raw or something. But still I don't cry . . . I sweat instead of crying. After a session with Greg I'm drenched . . . Pressure about my eyes, sweat pouring out my armpits. I go through 2 or 3 shirts a day, my brow is furrowed a lot, and I look at the ground as I walk."

My ability to see myself clearly, and my ability to fool myself.

"Unraveling. That is what I want. Let it all unravel."

The campus teemed with slender young men and women in shorts and T-shirts, yet sometimes in my memory the place seems stark and empty—blank, sunny expanses of white stucco or concrete or open fields, as schematic as the island of retired spies in *The Prisoner*.

"Sweat, sleep, eat, shit."

Voices outside my door, in the hall: "Gnarly . . . Killer . . ."

In my room, Fred called: "Destination: Moon."

Saturday night I danced "wildly" with E. in the quad, to "Rock Lobster"; saw Marya watching from the stoop of her dorm, in her big owl-ly glasses; felt elation turn to regret.

The Rock Lobster—life of the party, or angry outsider?

"Everybody dancin'. Everybody frugin'"—the perfect party, or outcast's nightmare?

Seeing the tragic in a B-52's song might be an aberrant reading, but so what.

I continued rereading the books on my list for my final oral exam, a requirement in my major.

"But that complexity and completeness that is holiness rests on the achievement of a level of human insight that is finally revealed by the poet to be a virtual impossibility," I wrote, of *The Faerie Queene.*

Possibility of sharing a place in San Francisco that summer with my high school friend Wayne, as we had done the previous summer in Berkeley.

Letter to another pal: "My friend E. has been telling me a lot about herself lately, and I'm always afraid that I will reject her."

I dreamed I compared cocks with the tall, sexy preppy who lived upstairs.

I reread the *Iliad.*

I forced myself to get involved with Liz, a girl in my dorm.

It was a drought year; "If it's yellow, let it mellow . . ."

"I have been getting closer to Liz . . . Mostly I like her because she listens to me so raptly . . . When, when, when will I simply like someone and pursue them?"

No one could sound more milquetoast than Fred growling that his love is "erupting."

I was attempting a new kind of Houdini trick—letting only half of myself out of my shell.

I reread Plato's *Apology.*

Day after day of sunshine and dry air; the hillsides were brown again by early May.

I wrote short stories about: the gay man who had been my boss at a summer job; an argument I had with E.; my mother's resentment toward my father; a sheriff whose brother loses his arm; my being chased by a bull, which I had dreamed.

The guy down the hall said to me, "Let's make a Liz sandwich," and I pretended to laugh.

The clear sky, the open horizon of the sea, and my amorphous inner blob of unhappiness, shame, frustration, rage, confusion.

The fiction teacher suggested my protagonist might be attracted to the character named Mike. I disagreed.

The odd nature of the closet, the open secret, not only to others but to oneself.

Periods of denial and periods of self-awareness.

"There's a moon in the sky. It's called the moon."

And yet by starting to write fiction that year, I had, in a way, already left Santa Cruz.

In the co-ed bathroom, after I had peed, E. said, in faux Southern accent, "I love a man with a strong urethra!"

In New York she would become my girlfriend, off and on, for three years—but that's another story.

I'm not describing a straight path toward anything.

"We're blessed, we're blessed, we're blessed, we're blessed," Chris sang one morning at breakfast, aping Tammy Faye Bakker.

As kids my brother Ken and I had often entertained each other with parody cartoons of bad TV dramas.

As far as I can tell, I barely spoke to Ken that year.

Letter from my high school friend Wayne telling me he was gay.

He was involved with a guy in Cambridge, so he wouldn't be moving to San Francisco for the summer after all.

Reply to Wayne, admitting, "I, too, have had feelings toward men."

I heard Liz's voice out in the hall, but didn't go out to talk to her.

Music as relief from continually having to choose and choose and choose.

The cymbal rolls like a gong as Fred calls, "Down, down!"— submarine, fellator, dreamer.

I tried to decide where to move after graduation, if not San Francisco.

I wondered what it would be like to have sex with Wayne.

I flipped to the black page in *Tristram Shandy*.

Every twenty-two-year-old is lost in the effort of formation, but some more than others—more secretive, more fumbling, more "from scratch," more thwarted, more hopeless, more undaunted, more against-all-odds.

Chris broke out giggling at the slightest sign of humor, so he was constantly saying, "Sorry. Sorry. Go on."

Chris also turned out to be gay, but that was later.

I reread *Sir Gawain and the Green Knight*.

Liz told me she had never met anyone so sensitive.

The fear of exposure, the self-ridicule, the inward no-no-no, the ickiness, the closed loop, the hope that somehow I *could* be different, the forced blooms of hetero desire, the sheer effort of it all, the constant expenditure of mental and emotional energy.

"Can you name, name, name, name them today?" sang Kate and Cindy on the morning of my exam.

In the book-lined office I took my seat before the three professors—and froze.

I couldn't seem to answer any of their questions.

At one point I said, "Am I getting warmer?"

"He was, however, clearly nervous," said the evaluation, "and this led to a self-consciousness in his answers that produced a rather blocked exam. There was a disappointing tentativeness to his performance—though he knew his texts, he had trouble deploying them in the exam context . . . When encouraged to develop a perspective he had thought through, he tended to lose the edge of his argument and become distracted and diffuse . . . He managed to convey an ability he did not fully demonstrate."

Afterwards, Mike comforted me over a beer.

Of Liz I wrote: "There is something missing—what is it?"

Whenever I told my therapist I might be gay, he threatened to send me to the gay counselor on staff.

Description of Liz: "She is Chinese. She has long hair, a face like a Gauguin. She is very insecure. But when we are just alone and talking, none of the negative matters."

Invitation from a friend in Texas to come live in Austin, where a guy she knew was making a movie that I could work on.

Describing a single B-52's song from start to finish would be like climbing inside a dream of my frustrated, secretive youth.

Regarding Liz: "I want to kiss her, I want to touch her. But there are blocks, blocks, BLOCKS. Obstacles."

"Can I ever stop pressuring myself to feel certain things?"

Tinny sixties organ, like some forgotten Morse code. "Remember," Cindy breathily confides, "when you held my hand." A succession of girl-group fragments. She's stuck in a world of clichés, seeking glamorous wisdom. I feel for Cindy—she's lost her man. The faint toy piano: generic scary-movie "insanity." At last the stock phrases give way to screams: "Why don't you dance with me? I'm not no limburger!" Comic but also kind of heartbreaking. She's only screaming like I wish I could. Fred chimes in now, the circus ringleader: "Dance this mess around!" Whipping up the animals, egging on the dream. The guitar insists, and now Kate tells of parties at which she, also a "mess," is danced around in various styles—"shy tuna . . . camel walk . . . hippy shake." I, too, knew the hippy shake—it could still be seen at parties in Santa Cruz, circa 1980. I, too, a mess—though never so artfully described as by Kate's trumpet-y soprano, slightly raspy, almost screechy—singing the title sentence over and over, in ever wilder melodies, as if in madness or abandon, while the others sing their "yeahs"—affirmation at last?

A cute guy from the dorm told me he freaked out on acid and saw a giant grasshopper up in a field.

Chris ran as a convention delegate for Ted Kennedy, who opposed Carter in the Democratic primary, but I voted for Chris out of personal loyalty rather than political zeal.

"All afternoon I was lying here trying to have a nap and feeling like I am breaking apart emotionally. Pressure on all sides: parents, school, myself, Liz, and finally my psychologist. For a moment I fell asleep, and a British voice said, 'Everyone accusing you. It's too much. Don't you think you need a pardon?'"

Fred's falsetto "British" accent: "Rock lobster?"

The phrase repeated over and over, as if it could mean anything—and does.

Another brief dream in which I wanted to saw my way across a bridge—destroying, going to a lot of trouble and turmoil for nothing, just to clear the way that was already clear.

"I wish my life would stop, so much happens . . . I have been getting closer to Liz sexually . . . I just looked out the window. It is a beautiful day—rainy, cloudy, some sun, and the grass is all brown . . . I love rain and cold in summertime."

I considered staying in Santa Cruz for the summer; I wondered if Liz being there was a plus or a minus.

Regarding Liz: "So we got to the shirt-taking-off point, and then she wanted to take my pants off and I just didn't want to . . . I'm beginning to feel like such a freak—cold, gay, whatever."

Despite the oral exam, I graduated with honors.

At the graduation ceremony, which was outdoors, a crazy woman from town named Cosmic Lady yelled from the back, "All right, all you mother-fuckers and father-fuckers!"

In the sunny courtyard I stood and smiled with my parents as an acquaintance took our photo.

Ken hadn't come up for the ceremony.

Evaluation for my fiction workshop: "His stories 'The Neptune Visitor' and 'The Mother' both tried to capture the tragedy of human alienation and the results were provocative. The language Cliff employed in most of his stories allowed for the narrative to take place on two levels, and even though this may not have been his intention, it worked well."

3

I MOVED MY stuff out of the dorm and back to my parents' house in San Jose.

At breakfast, the rubber-banded box of frozen sausages and the plastic bag of frozen diminutive corn muffins.

I rubbed our dog's floppy tan ears, which were whitish with age.

My father had retired two years earlier but my mother still worked part-time, as a bookkeeper for a music and arts center up in the hills.

"He just sits in his chair all day," she whispered.

During an argument over Christmas break, she had said to me, "Why are you shutting me out?"

I continued trying to decide what to do about Liz.

I went for a run—lawn, street, lawn, street, lawn, street, and scarcely a person to be seen.

All the houses made of stucco.

I considered visiting old teachers but decided against it.

I mowed while my father carefully trimmed along the sidewalk.

I napped on my old bed, feeling the perfect breeze that always blew through that house.

A summer dinner from childhood: corn on the cob, sliced ham, sliced tomatoes, and watermelon for dessert.

"Oh, that's good!" said my father.

Presumably he made cracks about nuking Iran, and presumably I ignored him.

The jasmine blooming along the fence under the window of the dining room.

The speckled whitish slightly bumpy linoleum under my feet.

"You knocked the heating register out of place," said my father, so I bent to fix it.

My parents sat watching TV, which I disdained.

I drove my mother's white boxy Dodge to the house of an old high school friend, and we went to see *The Shining*.

"Heeeere's Johnnie!"

In the darkened theater I began to shake uncontrollably.

When I got home, my parents had gone to bed and the house was dark.

"Tonight I saw the most frightening movie that I have ever seen in my life . . . I'm very upset. I'm even crying a little . . . I feel like I'm on LSD . . . When I came into the house—

suddenly I understood paranoia. Literally everything is potentially frightening, harmful. I just looked at the [blank] TV screen and the reflection in it and a chill went down my back . . . Mirrors or open doorways seem horrifying—what is to be seen in them? . . . The most frightening image: a hallucination he has. God, I almost can't say it . . . The man sees a beautiful woman get out of the bathtub. This is hurting me to talk about it. He embraces her, but when he looks in the mirror, he sees she is old, wrinkled, scabby. There. I'm through it . . . And I'm paranoid again; my heart is beating . . . I really feel like I'm going crazy. Or I see how people go crazy . . . God, it is awful to see these things in yourself . . . The world seems scabby, wrinkled. I'm afraid I'll start hallucinating. I keep telling myself that a movie can't hurt me. Actors, sets, film only . . ."

I woke my mother and we sat up talking at the dining room table; I told her how I felt pressured to be with Liz; my mother looked uneasy.

Still, she was a comfort to me that night.

A few days later I returned to Santa Cruz, where I found a share in a house not far from Mike's.

"I am feeling almost normal again but I'm still a little scared; and all the pressures that led up to that night are still there."

A dream in which my parents are unkind to me: "I just remembered the end . . . I ran into my room. Ken was there, and he was extremely understanding; his face was like a kindly Buddha or something. Of course that scares me . . . Yet I want to think about that face of Ken's . . . a refuge from all the accusation, irritation, lack of compassion, and frustration. I'm not sure what Ken symbolized."

How at any given moment you never quite know what life you're in the midst of hatching.

Whenever I moved anywhere, I always set up my stereo first.

There might have been a confrontation with Liz, or maybe I simply hoped not to run into her in town.

The ones Kate doesn't want, the ones who dance her around.

I would someday claim Fred's faggy voice as my own: record album as prophecy.

In listening again now, I pay homage to the sacred blind task of destroying and remaking myself.

The odd miracle of the needle in the groove.

The knitting quality of any music with a beat.

The knitting quality of the crackle of vinyl.

I've always loved songs that go through phases, such as when the guitar riff changes in "Rock Lobster" and an insect begins to croak.

I was becoming in some ways exactly what I wanted to be, and in other ways, exactly what I didn't want to be.

My room was at the front of the house, and instead of coming through the front door, Mike simply climbed in my window.

I got a temporary job working graveyard shift for Intel, testing chips.

Cathy wrote suggesting I move to New York, where she was working for the Strand bookstore.

Exhausted from my shift, I walked home along the water, under the early morning clouds.

Cindy singing "rock lobster" again and again, "operatically" —child imitating a diva, or mouse singing in an old cartoon.

The year I didn't lose my virginity; the year I learned to read—that is, ironically; the year I began writing fiction; the year I traded Joni Mitchell for the B-52's; the year I met Cathy, befriended Chris and E., and grew close to Mike; the year I nearly flunked; the year I lost my mind.

"But the future pops in my mind again," I wrote. "What do I want? I don't seem to know in the least."

AS IF

1

OUR FIRST NIGHT together, after a party in the East Village, E. and I undressed and simply lay side by side for a while, out there on the hide-a-bed in the living room.

The sound of the pita joint below, pots and pans banging.

"Touching is permitted," she said at last, with just the right amount of irony.

And so a key was turned.

"In a moment, our hands touched," I wrote the next day (October 30, 1981), "—at first, perhaps only a gesture before sleep, a gesture of great affection, as if we might have just gone to sleep holding hands."

Because of my inexperience and my indecision, I was too afraid to fuck.

The creaky brown sofa bed where we kissed, the orangey dark of the streetlight, and E.'s sighs.

My roommate Owen asleep behind the heavy curtain of his doorless room.

I had had a boyfriend the previous spring, and when I walked the streets alone, I glanced at guys.

Call her E., to spare her privacy, or because she's elemental, or because the initial alone sounds less charged, more objective, than what her name came to mean.

Even now, some combination of dread, embarrassment, and longing stops me after each sentence, and I have to take a breath.

We were together, off and on, for more than three years.

Her name is also a man's name.

But this isn't merely a story of sexual confusion, rather of self-doubt, which is bigger.

The auburn highlights in her hair, which she kept neck- or shoulder-length.

The way she flipped it around, comically but also sexily, her manner of flirting being mainly to parody coquetry.

For the next several weeks, E. and I continued our heavy petting.

Her slender torso and round bottom, the utter softness of her small conelike breasts.

At twenty-three my shyness about intercourse was a point of shame.

At twenty-three I was somehow both utterly vulnerable, and utterly closed.

Discovery of my finger on her wet button, and how it made her cry out.

We went to see an avant-garde play called *Mr. Dead and Mrs. Free*, which contained a rap song about fucking.

We walked arm in arm from the East Village to the West.

E. was not a virgin but she reassured me that our necking made her feel pleasantly like a teenager again.

She had moved to New York to find a job in publishing and now worked at *Rubber World*, a trade magazine. I had thought it unwise for her to take the position.

I wrote of not being "in love" with her, of "gaps" between us that were "hard to define."

E.'s department at work was called Fulfillment. Her many jokes about this.

My weariness of my own job, as the typist for a group of elderly journalists.

My gigantic blue IBM, an early word processor, with its dial of fifty memory slots like a kitchen timer.

I glanced through the *Times* each morning, but very little of the news penetrated.

I do recall reading the article titled "Rare Cancer Seen in 41 Homosexuals."

Example of the homophobia that was simply normal in 1981: my roommate Owen had not allowed me to kiss my boyfriend in front of him.

I kept gay themes out of the fiction I was writing.

My letters home in which I tried to explain myself, without explaining myself.

My many letters to friends, some sent, others not, some honest, some not.

My mother's curiously detailed letters from California that revealed nothing of her interior life.

My tenement street full of fire escapes.

One night I heard Owen arguing with his father on the phone; he hung up and screamed; I hesitated to go ask what had happened.

He was writing a movie script in which the protagonist has twenty-four hours to screw as many girls as possible before he gets married.

Janet, the other editorial assistant where I worked, openly disliked me, and my pal Leslie, the intern, had left.

Cathy, too, had left New York, and I now had virtually no friends there besides E.

She arrived an hour late for a movie. "I was so pissed waiting for her," I wrote, "but then when I saw her face, she looked so sheepish and beautiful [that] I melted."

It was chilly and she was wearing a white wool shawl—it's one of my fondest memories of her—but we didn't screw that night either.

My fear that intercourse with E. would be a "lie," either because I wasn't in love with her, or because I was "actually" queer.

"My poor oppressed little homosexual self," I wrote. "I keep 'realizing' it and 'realizing' it."

I developed a rash on my hand, where the pen rested.

At work I had to apologize to my boss for walking away, in anger, while he was still speaking to me.

Thus began the many years of asking myself how the hell I should support myself.

"My tongue in her mouth—I can't explain it, honestly, the feeling of—unity? Union? Closeness?" I wrote in my journal. "Union, I guess."

Even now, not knowing just where to put her in my mind.

The particular music of her voice, the wry arch of her eyebrows, like a prettier Imogene Coca.

"I felt my skin to be so at home against hers, my face against her neck," I wrote. "I feel self-forgiven and whole."

Meanwhile, I finished a short story that I was proud of.

The laundromat ladies squawking at me in their Monty Python voices to arrange my sheets around the agitator: "Circle! CIRCLE!"

The view up my street: Washington Square's arch; down my street: shimmery rectangles of the World Trade Center.

"I am a homosexual. I dream about men, I look at men, I fantasize about them," I wrote.

Of course it's only in retrospect that such statements look like clarity.

Other times I thought of my ex-boyfriend as merely an "experiment."

It's as if I wanted to make the choice as difficult for myself as possible.

Thanksgiving Day: E. on top of me, her breasts just brushing across my chest.

The sensation of first entering her.

2

IN MY JOURNAL I described fucking as a "roller coaster."

I wish I could look back on that period with "wry wisdom," with a twinkly smile at myself—which wasn't even myself, because I was so different then, and that was so long ago.

I still dream about E., periodically.

Recently she slipped over the edge of a terrace. I grabbed her pink hood, but she dropped out of the jacket and into the ice-cold sea below. Fortunately John dove in after her, pulling her to a small pebbly beach.

This sounds possibly redemptive, though it was unclear whether E. was still alive.

Her boyfriend before me had once slept with a guy too, she informed me—"Most intelligent men have."

She often made authoritative statements such as this.

"Brick House" came on; her whoop of pleasure; she ground down to the floor and back up again, hands clasped high above her head.

Her dance moves wild and mysterious to me.

Her bravado wild and mysterious to me.

"Too weird!" she liked to say, in delight.

Like Pigpen, I was creating my own cloud of obfuscating dust that traveled with me everywhere.

"Every choice seems to stamp out so many options, sides of me," I wrote. "... A hollowness in my stomach, a longing or a riddle."

My chest gradually sprouting light brown hairs.

On my turntable, Talking Heads' keyboard arpeggios: overlapping ripples in a shallow pool.

Satisfying whoosh of the old water tank above my toilet, and the weird porcelain shelf in the bowl, as if for inspecting one's stool before flushing.

That Christmas, in California, my mother lifted the pink nightgown from its splashy department store box, a gift from my father. "Ah," she said, pleased, and Ken took a picture.

The reason this tale is bigger than sexual preference is my mother.

The ways that being with E. resembled being the particular child of this particular mother.

My running argument with her over her complaints about my father.

The difficulty of even getting to her through the fog of her grudges.

Her stories about him went back years and years, and from childhood I'd been required to listen to them, or she'd withdraw.

And so it felt natural to put myself aside to get love.

Indeed my father could be selfish and impractical and the family had suffered certain misfortunes because of this.

My mother apparently believed that she had not only to tolerate resentment but actually to cultivate large fields of it, with the help of fertilizers and pesticides.

Over dinner she told of the mistakes and stupidity she had encountered at her bookkeeping job.

In turn Ken and I exchanged conspiratorial glances across the dish drainer, just as we'd done as kids, then ran to the back bedrooms as soon as possible.

Somehow Ken's coming out to me had only muddied my own sexual picture.

After my parents had gone to bed, he spoke to me of bars and "tricks" and the gym.

As opposed to my own nerd bohemia.

It took me a moment to realize that by "girlfriends" he meant male pals with whom he did not have sex.

My inability to imagine what my own gay life could be like.

Just the same, at a college friend's New Year's Eve party, in San Francisco, I danced with another guy, whom I described in my journal as "loose as a puppet."

"If there is such a thing as being 'true to yourself,'" I wrote on January 1, 1982, "sometimes it seems I must be brave and become gay."

3

DURING THE FLIGHT back to New York I observed beyond the wing a curious rainbow that formed a complete circle.

Wintry air smelling of rubber leaked into the jetway as I exited the plane.

The A train arrived covered in half-scrubbed-off bubble-letters.

Owen with his bushy black eyebrows threw aside the heavy curtain in the doorway to his room, like Dracula and his cape. "Hey."

He ate as usual with the TV on, accompanied by the pratfall music of *The Brady Bunch*.

Yet another set of rooms I wanted to escape; I called E. and went to her place.

Her eyes closed in laughter.

Small pert mouth, turned-up nose, brown eyes alight with amusement.

Her capacity for multiple orgasms.

Afterwards, she half moaned and half laughed, throatily, earthily.

"Oh, man," she said, playfully imitating a soul singer, but also meaning it.

I enjoyed the slightly sore feeling in my cock.

Her fixations on certain comic phrases, which matched precisely my own sense of humor.

Something dripped on me in the hallway of my building. "I felt wetness," I said to E. "Then, I smelled something." Pleasure of her raucous laughter. Pleasure of her repeating it over and over, for weeks.

"When she takes my cock in her hand," I wrote, "it makes me feel as if my soul fills all the crevices of my body."

I showed her how deep my navel is. "Too real!" she squawked.

Her black pumps, ruffled white socks, short flared black skirt.

Oddly sensual smell of the diaphragm cream, E. squatting on the floor to insert, thrill of knowing I'd soon follow—

Nostalgia, now, for that feeling.

The ways we meshed and the ways we did not, and how that combination enthralled me.

Her bubble of private jokes.

Her weird inability to listen, or was it my weird inability to speak my mind.

In my apartment I lay on my tiny bed with yet another cold.

I sat at my desk, typing on my Smith Corona.

I had made the desk from a door I found on the street, and it still smelled of urine whenever I cleaned it.

I asked my journal if I had any right to think of myself as a writer.

White roach powder all along the baseboards of the apartment—completely ineffective.

The layers and layers of shiny paint on the woodwork.

Owen's odd Egyptian-statue body, pale skin, patches of black hair at the navel and the middle of his chest, and deep-set almost black eyes behind dark horn-rims.

Marilyn Monroe appeared on his TV in a low-cut blouse as he ate; he gasped; I wondered if his sexuality was in any way like mine.

Settled into the orange shag I decoded gay-themed lyrics such as Chrissie Hynde's mournful reference to "things you never outgrow."

I walked the deserted streets of Soho past darkened ornate buildings.

In the darkness in my room, roach-legs lightly skittering across the walls.

E. declared that in college she had once "hallucinated wolves" in the darkness outside her third-floor window.

My fear of being sucked down into my own craziness by such tales.

Sometimes in the middle of a conversation she would start making bird noises.

Against my advice, she had taken a room in an apartment in Midtown with a French jazz musician in his forties. He leered at her and never laundered his towels.

We went to see *Night of the Iguana*. Afterwards she exclaimed, "Come on, have a nice rum coco!", in perfect imitation of Ava Gardner.

She also aped Gardner struggling with a screen door, then charging through, "in distress."

I rolled on her bed laughing. She did it again. I laughed and laughed.

Though our humor was in some ways evasive, it was also a genuine thing we had together.

The particular feeling of that dark room of hers in the East 60s, in winter.

A story E. told me: A mutual acquaintance from college said to her, regarding our romance, "But Cliff is gay." "Not with me, he isn't," she replied.

After five colds in less than two months, I was diagnosed with mononucleosis.

Already thin, I grew even thinner, which E. said was "sexy."

I lay day after day staring at the striped African cloth above my bed, trying to recover.

The swollen sore lumps under my jawline.

Regarding what it was like to hold my tall ex-boyfriend in my arms: "It was just too much," I confided in my journal, "—his size, his firmness, the hair on his face and body . . . a feeling of lushness. . . What a fine line I walk then as long as I stay with [E.]. And perhaps I feel I want to walk such a fine line all my life."

Constant hiss of the flesh-colored "DeVilbiss" humidifier, which E. and I called the Devil Bliss.

With velvet chords Steely Dan warned, "Soon you'll throw down your disguise."

Gradually the dull but stabbing pain in my right side—my spleen—began to pass.

"This morning when I woke up," I wrote, "I was joking with E. and I said, 'Where am I? When did I leave Anchorage?'"

4

TANGLED UP IN knots and trying to love.

E. grew dissatisfied with New York and moved back to California that spring. I stayed behind to attend graduate school, visiting her over the next year and a half in Santa Cruz, San Francisco, and Los Angeles. Then she moved to Boston to attend library school, and we began seeing each other regularly again. We broke up again. We considered getting back together again. It was now 1984.

Regarding my possibly being gay: "Her voice broke when she spoke of it—she said she would feel like she had 'failed' . . . she didn't know if her attachment to gay men was self-undermining."

Possibly she experienced the obscure satisfaction of winning me over, again and again.

I dreamed I got a job as a mathematician—the field that (in real life) Ken had chosen and I had rejected.

I often went out intending to go to a gay bar but ended up just walking the cold streets of the Village.

The homeless woman on Bleecker, naked from the waist up, holding one breast in each hand and loudly singing, "Sweet dreams are made of this."

Ronald Reagan had famously blamed homelessness on the homeless, but I wasn't thinking in political terms just then.

Of my dilemma, the secretary at work said, "Cliffy just doesn't know where to put it."

In my playwriting workshop, the actors read my scene in which we hear the protagonist's thoughts, but there's no one on stage.

The instructor stopped the reading. "Wait a minute. Am I misreading this? The stage is empty?" "Yes," I said. The class laughed. I blushed.

Afterwards a tall dark-haired guy in the class named Gerson consoled me.

Dream: ". . . Then, for the sort of vague reason that means it's time for the show to end, they go and look under the monster's rock (from where he grabbed victims) and he wasn't there."

I wondered in my journal if breaking up with E. had been "like breaking up with myself."

I closed my eyes as Prince proposed harpsichord-like synthesizer as the sound of doves crying.

I told my friend Mike, "I have the sensation of a hold button for her blinking in my head."

I wrote, "Did I push her away for *any* good reason?"

At the time, each turn in my labyrinth seemed significant.

Light-filled rain, finches chirping, bundles of daffodils at the corner market.

"Intense eye contact" with a blond man on the subway, aborted by the man running into a friend.

Up at school I averted my eyes from my teacher, Grace Paley, "not from dislike or pride, but from fear."

Grace had correctly identified my new short story about Mike as "an unconsummated love story."

I went to playwriting class and there was no one there, and no sign that class had been canceled.

The nonprofit organization I worked for went under.

A "cylindrical pain" in my throat.

My friend Gabby remarked that I never got angry.

Thoughts on my play: "[The protagonist] appears, but cannot speak; he is spoken to as if present, but is not; only parts of his body can be seen; he speaks in sync to recorded voice-over (in the 'love scene'); he floats suspended over those scenes he doesn't participate in."

I cleaned out my desk at work.

Grace smiled at me at a party at school, and I wondered if she knew what a mess I was.

I went to her apartment for a conference, and when she said, "Do you want an egg? I'll make you an egg," I mainly wondered when the other shoe would drop.

I still dream about Grace from time to time, which seems to be the same as dreaming about my mother.

More abortive cruising on the streets of the Village.

A dream that my father died but no one wanted me to cry, because I'd never liked him.

Description of a boss at a temp job: "She smiles as she asks you to please wipe her ass for her. Then she asks you to please double check and make sure it's clean."

Of a short story of mine, a magazine editor wrote: "We don't understand it."

I dreamed that I watched my college friend Chris and his father dance the rumba.

"Only moments," I wrote, "never a sense of whole days lived."

5

IN JULY I went to see E. in Boston: "[We] fucked four or five times in two days, and I didn't come once. At one point she thought I had, and she burst into tears. I felt like everything is lost as soon as it's found."

Her fits of panic, raucous laughter, difficult tales of childhood, professions of love.

As she tried to draw my attention to a squirrel flicking its tail in the park, I thought, "How am I going to get through the weekend?"

She often told of meeting crazy people who told her horrific stories.

Extracting love from me must have been like pulling teeth, and I, too, was trying to extract it from myself.

How special it was when my mother's sun shined on me.

"I opened the living room window and this rush of cool, scented air greeted me," I wrote. "The birds are singing. I can hear the stereo downstairs. There's a laziness to the street sounds; it's early: a few voices, an occasional car, squeaking brakes; faint roar of traffic in the distance."

Gerson, from playwriting class, took off his glasses as we talked over lunch, and I hoped this meant he was attracted to me.

I dreamed my father was a heroin addict.

E. visited me in New York. Insert difficult scenes here.

Fucking her—that indescribable hand-in-glove feeling, that is, when I wasn't dreading impotence.

She called to say she wanted to quit library school and move back to New York.

I felt like I couldn't breathe.

I went to the beach, ostensibly to think but actually to look at men.

My therapist at the time was no help whatsoever, yet I continued seeing him twice a week.

In a short story I referred to him as "Bela Lugosi."

I began to hate E.'s perfume.

My friend Gabby said I was "warm on three sides, ice on one."

I dreamed that a cute guy from school said, "I brought a present for you," and gave me a hotdog from his freezer.

On the phone with E. I pointed out that she hated New York.

I added that I didn't know how I felt about her, which predictably made her angry.

I complained in my journal about constantly having to "nursemaid" her, about her many tales of stomach upsets on the bus, nerves on the subway, at work . . .

"I just glanced at the floor: a roach going by a dustball."

Michael Stipe rasped-crooned, "What is dreaming?"

Morrissey crooned-shrieked "Ah!" as if goosed.

I walked all over the Village again and the next morning my right heel really hurt.

I removed my sock to reveal a red spot the size of a quarter, on the left side near the instep.

I broke a molar.

From a short story I was writing: "While the Jamaican assistant vacuumed [his mouth], the dentist chipped and drilled away at his [broken] tooth. It didn't seem like much, but at home a look in the mirror, open wide—half a molar gone. 'Frightening,' he said out loud. 'Jesus.' He called his parents in California. 'It's a very common bad dream, universal in fact,' he said, '—loosing your teeth, that is.' *But then, they don't have any teeth at all, so what am I doing complaining to them?* The temporary filling a bad medicine taste in the mouth for days and days."

The root canal I had had the year before was unsuccessful and I would need oral surgery.

I received my first acceptance of a short story, by a small journal.

I found $200 hidden in my thesaurus.

"I told [E.] that her dramatic life was too much for me sometimes . . . She said, crying, that she's been in love with me for three years . . . I don't know how much I believe that."

I got a temporary job as a secretary at the magazine where I would work for the next twenty-four years.

A handsome man in the building made eyes at me.

D train barreling down the tunnel from 34th to 4th, bouncing and clacking, lights a-flicker.

Regarding my writing: "All my stories scare me. I write one paragraph and put it away. Every one of them is about homosexuality, except one, which is about E. and therefore probably about homosexuality."

My oral surgeon was also named Cliff.

"He put the gas on me, oxygen at first, which made me laugh a little, then laughing gas, which made me feel as though I couldn't breathe and yet I was powerless, adrenaline pumping and my heart pounding, and I was afraid I wouldn't calm down for the operation, nor could I move; then the injection and blacking out, sounds echoing—literally reverberating, and me saying to myself a prayer I feared I'd be unable to finish, and I feared being unable to think again, so I told myself a joke, 'I'm . . . falling . . . asleep . . . and . . . I . . . will . . . wake . . . up . . . someday . . . and . . . be . . . a . . . better . . . person . . . for . . . it.' From the sludgy blackness I heard the doctor calling, 'Cliff . . . Cliff . . . Cliff . . . Cliff? Howyadoin'?'"

6

AS IF THE whole romance were an extended metaphor that got less and less tenable as the story dragged on for three whole years. As if love and sex were a matter of suspending disbelief. As if purely physical sensation were enough. As if I don't miss that sensation. As if I could have continued the experiment indefinitely. As if I could ever forget her. As if I could place myself squarely at a single point on some "sexual preference" continuum. As if the blurry, indistinct facts weren't still facts. As if she were my mother asking me to forget my father and take care of her. As if all the love between us meant nothing compared to my attraction to men. As if the snow and the cold outside her window were sent to make the warmth of her bed seem even more delicious. As if the newness of cold and snow could make me a new person. As if my childhood sensation of doom could ever become a comfy homey glow. As if my cock inside her were all of me inside her. As if my whole body and maybe even my soul had entered paradise. As if our laughter afterwards were the chirping of paradisiacal birds in a winter of fire escapes and smudged windows overlooking airshafts. As if playfulness alone could sustain us. As if I could distance myself from her now by placing her in some realm apart from every relationship since. As if she were indeed a bird I had bedded in some fable set in a city of castles. As if that trapped feeling I had were simply "normal." As if lying to myself and to her were harmless. As if I could keep these memories at bay by getting metaphoric. As if I could begin to sum up what she meant or means to me. As if at last I were finally getting my mother's complete devotion. As if at last I were getting all the happy romance I'd envied throughout my crimped homo youth. As if she were the open backdoor to my closet, onto another world, surreal and magical, where time stops or at least slows and we wander naked and "free" on the grassy hillsides of fiction. As if her reminding me of my mother were "normal." As if I could ever know what her own myths and lies were. As if her having her own reasons could absolve mine. As if she had only crazy reasons. As if by not thinking about her all these years I was building up antibodies to the pained confusion that permeates these memories, a feeling that still arises in dreams about her. As if I could ever reconcile the good and the bad in our romance, both of which were extreme as well as firsts in my life. As if you could ever get to the bottom of desire. As if I could ever lay to rest the mystery of any two people in love. As if with the words "doomed nature" I could explain our love to myself. As if all these "as if's" could explain it.

7

ON THE PHONE E. told me I was judgmental and that I had "no interest in her life," both of which were true.

She also said she had indigestion, she'd stayed home from work and spent the day crying.

I lay in bed with a low-grade fever.

I wrote, "She'll never be happy until I say, 'I love you.'"

I speculated that my feelings toward men might be "an effort to get my father back," though I speculated further that this theory might be completely wrong.

E. sent me a short story about picking a favorite stuffed animal, "always with plastic moving eyes," to join her in her card-table fort, then feeling sorry for the others she hadn't picked.

"But when I begin to feel like I should call it off," I wrote, "E. seems such a lost precious thing to me, such a lovely, wonderful thing."

She came to New York and we had a "surprisingly good" weekend together.

A few days later I wrote, "I can't *deal* with her crying."

A straight friend called to tell me she had run into my ex-boyfriend in Seattle; she described him as "a narcissistic jerk" and "really faggy."

I wrote, "I act a little faggy sometimes and I hate fearing judgment for it."

In the short story I was writing, I compared visiting E. to riding my bicycle to see a girlfriend in junior high: ". . . pedaling in the heat—the body growing shaky and sweaty—past long rows of spinach in spreading fields, old silos, unidentifiable orchards: something like country lay between his house and hers."

I had a nightmare about a little girl who either was, or thought she was, the reincarnation of her grandfather; various cracked interpretations of the dream, including "I'm deeply afraid of genuinely looking forward to seeing E."

". . . wildly attracted to men all week."

My office at the magazine was on the very top floor of the building, under a peaked roof, with a view down Madison Avenue—slot canyon in summer haze.

I wrote: "Chris looked up from the plain white surface of his desk and saw his boss standing there, towering over him, a big blue suit wanting something . . . His boss nodded toward the empty desktop, smiling aggressively. 'Bored, huh?'"

One Friday when E. was visiting, this same boss came in to find her sitting in my guest chair, near tears, in her dowdy library school clothes; I blushed deeply.

I was ashamed of not just that moment but all of it—the whole damn three years.

As I waited with her at Grand Central for her train back to Boston, I sat reading an article titled "AIDS Victims at Greater Risk from Cancer, Doctors Report."

Following her visit: "Every time I heard a song that E. and I heard over the weekend, or every time anything reminded me of E., I would feel like I had just banged a leg on the same bruise."

Even now I can't listen to "Purple Rain."

David Byrne made "flippy floppy," and the electric violin moaned like a whale.

"Elaine just put her arms around him limply and said he didn't look real. He supposed this was true," I wrote. "Later she began to cry while they were making love, and Chris felt ashamed as he held her shaking ribs in his hands: again he had said maybe they should stop seeing each other."

Gabby said, "You're not going to marry her, are you?"

Cathy visited over Labor Day and I slept with her.

I informed E. of this and, predictably, she was angry.

In a letter she described seeing "white flashes every few seconds" when she thought of me with Cathy.

The letter went on to fantasize about our having a child together. The child comes into the living room and asks us to turn the music down so she can finish her homework.

This enraged me.

Phone conversation: "I meant . . . ," E. began. "What?" I shouted; "What? *What?* WHAT?"

Gabby said to me, wisely, "Ambivalence takes the greatest offense."

Up at school, Elizabeth Hardwick declared that one must foster an "almost demonic" self-criticism.

At the pasta store I watched the ancient machine chop the flat, green dough into linguini.

Journal: "A leaf fell and hit me in the face as I was explaining to Gabby how much I hated fall."

The podiatrist was baffled by the painful red spot on my right heel. He poked at it. "It's hot!" he said.

I wrote: "Chris explained that normally it was his other foot that hurt, almost all the time. The doctor poked around that foot for a while in various ways. Holding the foot tenderly, he looked up at Chris and said, 'Does this remind you of anything?'"

Eventually I was diagnosed with "reactive arthritis," for which I've taken medication ever since.

On the phone I told E. she was full of shit.

"You go from one trail of tears to the next," I said.

"Mental block," I wrote: "I don't understand her missing me so."

Gabby suggested I needed either to "go for it" with E. or break up and see someone new.

Dream: my friend Mike lifted me up and carried me as he flew.

Dream: I was "frenching" my old dog Sam.

My apartment: "My sweaters are heaped in the chair on the rumpled quilt, on the edge of this unmade bed. A mess on my desk, of papers and bug husks."

Dream that I had sex, at last, with a junior high crush: "I took his slender, bare, firm shoulders in my hands and we showered together."

I seemed to be willing each moment of the dream.

8

WRITING ABOUT E. is like revisiting the Old Country.

Examining all I had to leave behind in order to move forward, and fearing I'll get mired in it again.

On the train to Boston: "Stray landmarks go by in the darkness: a neon sign, block letters arranged vertically. New England depresses me."

On the Cape: "She just kept talking and talking and saying, 'I can't take it in. I can't take it in.'"

It's as if I had to complete all the required coursework in math before I could be sure I didn't want to major in math.

In Truro I turned our rented Chevy directly in front of another car, and we nearly collided. E. and I continued on to the youth hostel, stopping at some point to walk through a forest of stunted pines. We lay down on the needles and fucked. When I came, she burst into tears. I pulled up my pants feeling like a rapist, and just then a pack of motocross riders sped past on either side of us and disappeared into the woods again, engines revving. We went on to the dilapidated youth hostel, which as it turned out was closed for the season, but the handsome proprietor relented and let us stay. E. and I lay together in the lower cot of a rough bunk bed, shivering.

But my last night in Boston, we had "the most amazing sex I've ever had," I wrote. "We had had a bad day . . . We lay talking for an hour or more. Then suddenly I rolled over on my back and she climbed on top of me—and never has her skin felt so smooth. We both felt smooth instead of nervous and sticky. We kissed and when I began touching her clitoris I felt some new desire to be inside her—she seemed so wet and so desirable. After a while she put in her diaphragm and it was actually frustrating that she decided to go down on me. Finally she climbed on top of me again and I entered her. *Never has her vagina felt that way.* So smooth and soft and fine . . . Afterwards E. told me she had hallucinated butterflies."

I added that "my belief that I'm 'really' this or that"—homo or hetero—was "ridiculous."

Underneath it all, the mucky conviction that any price I had to pay for such sweetness was well worth it.

Similarly, the doom of trying to love my mother through her elusiveness—her resentments and frustrations, her airs and insecurities, her frosted wig and her violin, her playfulness and delight, her short temper, and the tender way she called me "Sweetie."

Yet also *not* wanting it at any cost.

That fundamental loneliness in me, and how it played out with E.

Recent memory of Mom's playfulness: she looks at me gingerly and quickly pops a cracker in her mouth, as if sneaking it.

It's like I could find the whole world of her love in that moment.

Thinking about E., I feel beaten down all over again.

Thinking about E., I want to run away from my life now, in case I'm still that mistaken.

Climbing back inside my "misspent youth."

Inside these stanzas of delusion.

Inside her.

Pure sensation, an iridescent texture, purple-green, like the neck of a mallard, glossy and firm, halted there just for you, gliding and turning slowly so you can observe each shifting color, though not merely a surface but dense, both delicate and dense, as if I were burrowing through a mound of pure pigment—

It's possible that my profound unhappiness with her even heightened the pleasure.

At such times I was like a cell accepting her, another cell, right into my protoplasm.

9

OVER BRUNCH, GABBY said I'd never opened up, as far as she knew, "for more than twenty minutes at a time."

After brunch: "It began to rain in heavy splashes and spurts as we left [the restaurant]. I wanted to preserve the moment . . . The sky was patchy and ragged with waves of clouds; we kept stopping in doorways to avoid a downpour—huge drops here, then there, across the street, suddenly the sky full of light, then dark again . . . By the time we got to her place we were soaked; we changed, read the paper, drank soda, listened to a tape, and the intensity of the afternoon drained away."

Yet another phone argument with E.: "She began to cry. She said if she opens up, just as things are going well I'll end it, out of some idea that ending it is an act of strength . . . She said I treat her like an 'experiment.'"

Indeed maybe I was trying to prove to myself over and over that I could leave her, even as I was trying to prove to myself that I couldn't.

My relationship with her was a kind of contraption or incantation, a cracked sense of cause and effect as in a dream.

"She said she 'can't read me,'" I wrote, "that I just say 'uh-huh' when she says things like 'I feel like you don't want me to move to New York.'"

The card I sent her that bore no message, only a burst of cartoon rays, emanating from a blank.

"Outside, that bright gray light just before a rain. The feeling that even in New York one can be at peace with the seasons. A horn, a truck motor down the street. The sky growing darker and duller. I lay on my bed—I sit here now—with a pain or pressure in my chest, the expectation of some doom. Rain, will you?"

Letter from E. consisting almost solely of instructions for cooking our Thanksgiving dinner.

Elizabeth Hardwick sat beside me in her office and together we read through my new short story.

"Chris was sitting with a book in the sun in the living room. *And I am telling you,* he said to himself, *desire is a burden. It is a burden, an arduous journey through spinach fields on a bicycle in the hazy heat of summer. I'm telling you and don't you forget it.*"

Elizabeth suggested only minor changes. Later she told my friend Erin, "Cliff Chase is a survivor."

Since then I've often thought about that statement.

Thanksgiving morning, before E.'s arrival, a vivid dream of kissing my mother's cheek, her face described in my journal as "overly palpable."

I cooked the Cornish hens as directed, she arrived from Boston, and we ate them. At some point we had sex. We went to a movie, sat together in various restaurants and coffee shops. We talked endlessly about the relationship. I continued feeling miserably trapped.

The strange *rightness* of feeling obliterated.

The weird pleasure of fooling yourself, like performing a magic trick in private, over and over—as if you could be surprised by your own sleight of hand.

William James: "There is no more miserable human being than one in whom nothing is habitual but indecision."

She missed her flight home Monday morning and returned to my apartment. I had already gone to work. She sat in her coat watching TV with Owen for an hour, hesitating to call me to say she had fucked up getting to the airport on time. We met for lunch. She was looking more and more bedraggled. In the diner she began to cry as she talked of hating library school, where she felt unappreciated. She said, "No one wants what I have to give." She cried again when she left for the airport. That night when she called from Boston, I broke up with her.

To call this decision "coming out" doesn't begin to describe it—though that's how I would simplify it later.

For months I agonized over whether we should get back together, and our discussions continued until April, when E. sent all my letters back to me.

Perhaps wisely, perhaps selfishly, I did not reply.

I sought the lugubrious advice of Tears for Fears.

Journal: "I want a record of it—of the texture of her vagina; of the play of our hips against each other; of my finger running over her clitoris under the little wet hood . . ."

I hadn't left E. because of some greater understanding of myself, but rather because I needed to do *something*.

Even now, some part of me believes I turned away love forever.

My mother was a frugal woman, and similarly I try not to discard any sort of affection that comes my way.

All the hilarious things E. said.

The way she looked in her white shawl, that night she was late to the movie.

"What we have is beautiful," she said to me, crying, on the phone. "Why do you want to kill it?"

EGYPT, IN ONE SENSE

1

SOLDIERS WITH MACHINE guns surrounded the plane as we filed down the tarmac in the balmy floodlit night.

Vast old terrazzo floor of the terminal; find the line for currency, then visas; guidebook warnings of graft; my fear of error; the brusque yet unhurried little clerk carefully making tiny marks on his forms, as if Arabic were a dream language; released at last into the balmy night air again and the new perils of dishonest taxi drivers.

For sometime I had been harboring panicky thoughts about John, such as, "We've been together four years and I still don't have a key to his apartment!"

As the reader may have noticed, I like to mingle love with panic, self-doubt, and conjecture.

Coming out hadn't solved everything.

The taxi sped noisily along the elevated highway wedged between plaster orange-lit buildings, and though the road was certainly no worse than, say, the Brooklyn-Queens Expressway, it all felt utterly makeshift, about to collapse, yet not collapsing, maybe suspended mid-collapse, and every window and roof and dark alley appeared in some fundamental way *different* from anything I'd ever seen before, and my capacity for astonishment awakened.

The first time John had ever spoken to me was in astonishment—we were standing next to a small pond in early spring listening to weird-sounding frogs—"Wow," he said, and I knew I wanted to know him.

Just as now we exchanged glances again and again in the cab.

Here, the space between sentences might suggest the gap between the part of me that was happy with John and the part of me that wasn't.

Gigantic billboards around the traffic circle advertised Egyptian movies with gigantic hand-painted faces of Egyptian movie stars.

Odor of unregulated car exhaust; frenetic plinking on the taxi radio.

The hotel appeared not to have been renovated since the 1920s and exuded a shabby colonial glamour: intricate wrought-iron gate; two-tier lobby chandelier, also wrought iron; dusty ornate carpet runner flanked by heavy, carved thrones.

Poker-faced handsome lobby clerk with Coptic cross tattoo on forearm.

I strongly suspected John had slept around in New York while I was away for three weeks earlier that summer, but I had said nothing.

We had tried couples therapy the previous year, but I never did get that key to his apartment.

I had been with G., my previous boyfriend, just about four years, of which I now saw the final three as wasted time.

John and I smiled at one another as we ascended the creaky steps, and again as we entered our huge dilapidated room with its tall shutters, worn red velvet drapes, tiled floor, and sagging maroon twin beds with massive dark-wood head-boards.

I had decided I wanted to go back to our couples counselor, but I had put off telling John.

I hoped that our vacation in Egypt—far from ordinary distractions—would be a good time to talk about it.

Muffled sounds of motorcycles, horns, footsteps, people shouting.

"I feel strangely at home here," I said, lying on my back and looking up at the cracked ceiling. "Me too," John said.

2

INDEED CAIRO OFFERED no ordinary distractions, only extra-ordinary ones.

We spent most of the next day with Abdul and Ali, a pair of young men who befriended us on the street as we puzzled over a map. They helped us 1) find the American Express office; 2) make our train reservations to Aswan for later in the week; 3) get our passport-size photos taken; 4) obtain fake student ID's so we could save money on the already low entrance fees to museums and other sights.

John and I were poorer back then, but not that poor. Nor were we students. I was thirty-nine and John was thirty.

I had caught a bad cold in Israel and was still jetlagged, thus I actually believed that these two friendly Egyptians were art students, that they were brothers, and that their names were indeed Abdul and Ali.

As soon as we accepted their aid, it was as if we entered a tunnel of gradually deepening trust.

Theory: Because my mother felt my father never listened to her, I doubted John could ever listen to me.

My mother's own disinclination to listen must also be taken into account.

Though John and I flattered ourselves that we were setting out on a fascinating cross-cultural friendship with Abdul and Ali, we tried numerous times to get rid of them by offering baksheesh, but they wouldn't hear of it.

Like all good confidence men they kept each of us engaged separately in conversation, so that we never had the opportunity to compare notes.

John and I did, however, exchange glances at Abdul's suggestion to go to his uncle's papyrus-painting shop, since we hoped this was what the two men had wanted all along, a commission on whatever we bought.

In the dim room we gazed at dozens of colorful images of pharaohs, barges, and various gods inked onto brown crinkly paper guaranteed to be real papyrus, not banana leaf.

"Did you paint any of them?" I naïvely asked, but Ali said no, they were still learning.

In our foolish parsimony, John and I bought only a single small painting, and thus began our next escapade: I agreed to go to the duty-free shop to purchase two bottles of liquor for Abdul.

The circuitous journey of that day must have rhymed with my perplexity over John, since that's the only way I can account for my continuing fascination with the incident.

Like my mother, I have a special talent for feeling cheated and deceived, whether of goods, services, or affection.

Until then John and I had walked everywhere with Abdul and Ali, but now as we rode in a cab with Abdul around a huge, insanely busy traffic circle, John glanced at me uneasily, and I realized with a bolt of dread that we had no idea where Abdul had asked the driver to take us or what might happen when we got there.

It wasn't a comforting portent that Ali, the gentler of the two, had decided not to join us on this errand.

But soon enough the taxi came to a stop in front of an ordinary-looking building, and Abdul led us upstairs to a store stacked to the ceiling with boxes; he spoke to one of the men behind the glass counter, and we were ushered into a side room to fill out the paperwork.

Something about the way the head-scarfed girl looked at me, as she made notations on my passport, caused me to ask just what I was signing up for.

"Twelve bottles whiskey," she answered, "twelve bottles vodka, two boombox—"

"No, no, no!" I said, with outsize indignation, and with equal flourish she tore the forms in two before my eyes.

Abdul had remained chatting with the men at the counter, so John and I tore out of there and hopped in a taxi, hoping Abdul hadn't seen us.

I knew from the guidebook that foreigners were restricted to four bottles of liquor each, and I could only guess what sort of fine or duty I'd have to pay at the airport—not to mention the boomboxes; I also knew that such things could be sold for a huge profit on the black market, and I feared being implicated in the crime.

As it happened, the taxi had to circle back past the duty-free store, where of course Abdul waved us to a halt.

"I come with you," he said, trying to open the door.

"No!" John shouted.

"*Fuck* you!" he yelled back. "I waste all my time on you."

Intense shame as John and I drove off—for running away from Abdul; for being fooled by him; for denying him his payoff.

Indeed, from a political standpoint (as well as a literary one), my sympathy tended toward the young unemployed Egyptian rather than the two Western tourists—or did I identify with Abdul for other reasons?

That day I never had a minute to worry over my feelings toward John.

Back at the hotel we talked about the encounter late into the night, trying to understand (for instance) whether I was signing up to actually pay for all that merchandise, or merely lending my foreign passport to the transaction; and who would resell the items, Abdul or one of the guys in the store?

We also wondered how we'd missed various warning signs that, back in New York, would have been perfectly obvious, or what we could have done differently to avoid the unpleasant scene in the taxi.

Perhaps most puzzling was that Abdul appeared genuinely hurt and betrayed by our getaway.

It occurs to me now that he must have felt humiliated in front of the store clerks.

At last John said, sighing, "He wasn't going to be happy no matter what we offered him. The whole thing was bound to end in tears."

John dislikes unpleasantness nearly as much as I do.

3

DUSTY CRUMBLING BUILDINGS in hazy morning light.

Huge wooden trays of fresh tan pita carried on bicycles through the streets.

I drank the fruit juice despite the ice, even though the guide-book had warned us not to; John frowned.

The old telephones in wooden stalls took only older Egyptian coins, difficult to obtain since they were no longer in general circulation, nor did my phone card work, so we failed at calling Gabby back in Israel.

The magical nature of the place, added to our desire to see it as such.

In the brand-new subway station two heavily veiled women giggled in delight as they stepped onto the escalator—evidently their first escalator ride—and so John and I also giggled in delight.

Of course we were ignoring political realities such as corruption and headlong urbanization.

I went back to the hotel to rest, but John didn't want to. I wrote in my journal that I wasn't feeling "in love" with him.

The hopeless all-or-nothing flavor of my distress at such moments, experienced not only with John but everyone I've ever been with.

My throat was sore and my nose required constant wiping.

Behind the shutters and velvet drapes: bright hazy air, rubble sidewalks, and the blaring call to prayer.

Were John and I bound to end in tears?

To complete my suffering, I inserted Joni Mitchell into my Walkman.

The Egyptian tissues were speckled and slightly scratchy. I briefly slept.

That night, the tower restaurant revolved uneasily on its Soviet-engineered track, creaking and lurching like an old ride at Coney Island.

"Cairo is to New York as New York is to San Francisco!" I said, referring to degrees of urban chaos.

Turning and turning with impossible smoothness, the dervish lifted his wide, multicolored skirt to form an inverted cone around his head.

I avoid conflict and see dilemmas everywhere.

Typical complaint of my mother's: "Dad doesn't like to do *x*, but I do."

I wondered if John and I were "just too different," for instance his rarely needing to go back to the hotel and rest, whereas I—

And there was the nine-year age gap, which seemed important then, less and less important in the many years since.

In a café or a mausoleum or a mosque, the place pouring into my senses, pouring into John's senses, pouring into our senses together.

The lit-up streets full of men, the bright tacky shops brimming with goods: we went into a toy store and bought an Egyptian version of Clue.

Of the dervishes I wrote, "Ecstasy is an action, not a state of being."

4

LIKE A CARTOON car the little taxi seemed to suck in its sides for the tightest passages, then bounce back to normal size, as we motored through Cairo's slums. The driver slowed for a battered pickup piled ten or twelve feet high with roughly hewn furniture. It stopped to unload a table, and though the alley had scarcely widened, once again our Fiat squeezed through and we accelerated into the next crooked channel. The driver achieved all this antic motion through no apparent effort, one palm resting lightly on the steering wheel, the other resting just as lightly on the gearshift. The trip lasted perhaps fifteen minutes but like a roller coaster ride seemed to go on and on. Powdery bright sunshine and blue black shade, motorbikes, donkeys, beat-up vans, men and children and covered-up women in dusty gowns pressing themselves against the flaking windowless walls as we sped by. We burst into a small ruined square, where suddenly a thriving produce market revealed itself—tomatoes, greens of all kinds, brown-flecked yellow tamarinds, bananas in various sizes, all laid out on plastic tarps amid the rubble. We rumbled on into another darkened alley, where a slender woman draped in cloth floated ahead of us, a lettuce the size of a basketball atop her head. John and I looked at one another in amazement. I comprehended the poverty, but "poverty" hardly described the profusion of daily life, in all its resourcefulness, flickering past our windshield.

Whether in rebuke or simply as the next twist of the kaleidoscope, the Mosque of Ibn Tulun—our destination—was as stark as a de Chirico.

Fortress-like walls surrounded a vast courtyard, a stairway circling the small minaret.

Inside, we were greeted by a small boy with eyes as huge as those in a velvet painting, who asked to be our guide by saying, "Guide?" and pointing to himself.

His tour was as minimal as the building itself. "Carrrving," he announced, pointing upward to the intricate stone archway of the colonnade in which we stood. He drew our attention to other features such as "courtyard" and more "carving."

"View," he said, unhooking the chain and leading us up the winding staircase.

There was an austere pleasure in learning absolutely nothing about the place beyond what we could see for ourselves. Like silhouettes in a line drawing, John and I squinted at the courtyard, the walkways above the four colonnades, the domed structure in the middle, all dusty and sand-colored, as if made of sand.

"Citadel," the boy said, pointing in that direction over the city. John and I had just come from there, so it was the one landmark besides the pyramids that we already knew.

Down the winding steps, we each gave the boy twenty pounds for the tour. He looked disappointed, so John also handed him his Bic lighter.

I frowned, as if John had gone way overboard.

"I wish there was some kind of rule," I said, getting into another cab. "Tip adults this and children that—so I wouldn't have to go around constantly doubting myself."

5

THAT NIGHT GABBY arrived from Israel, where she was living that year.

In Cairo's huge labyrinthine marketplace, John went off to explore while Gabby and I sat down in a gaudily tiled tourist café.

There I ordered the meal that would make me sick for the next year and a half.

"I saw your eyes in a portrait in the Coptic museum today," I said to Gabby. "That's uncanny," she replied, "because people keep commenting about my eyes lately!" At that moment everything seemed uncanny to me, probably due to my Egyptian cold medicine, Flu-Calm, which despite its name made my heart race. As did the strong tea I was drinking.

Gabby and I spoke of déjà vu, past lives, destiny . . . The food arrived. I had ordered Egyptian Pancake with Egyptian Hotdog, which I'd hoped was tourist-speak for a crepe with merguez, but in fact it was a flat doughy thing studded with orange chunks.

Doggedly I ate it.

The analogy might be my doggedly conducting my romantic life as I always had.

Gabby and I realized we had been talking a long time and John hadn't yet returned. I sipped my tea and began to worry.

Café noise, fluorescent lights, sugary odor of flavored tobacco; outside, the crowded square was strung with bare lightbulbs.

I silently fumed over all the other times John had been late.

But at last he arrived, breathless and exhilarated from having been lost in the innumerable winding passageways of the Khan al-Khalili. He sat down and told us about it. At first he was simply following his wonder, past the dozens of tourist shops full of perfume bottles, silver, or inlaid wood, and on into the real market—piles of baby clothes, towels, surplus plumbing fixtures, tools—until he realized everything was closing and the narrow streets were becoming more and more dark and deserted. He didn't know the language and didn't know where he was. Then he felt a hand firmly grasp his arm. He looked to see a teenage boy, who silently led him back through the maze to the brightly lit square. "Do you want to meet my friends?" John asked him, but whether or not the boy understood, he shook his head and disappeared again down the curving alley.

John's capacity for such adventures was something I'd always loved about him.

6

IN THE MIDDLE of the night I sat in the stained marble hotel bathroom shitting my brains out.

I say brains because I had entered an altered mental as well as physical state, a whirligig of alarm that had begun spewing inside my skull all the recent doubt and confusion over John.

"Are you OK?" he called through the door. "No," I said.

The sagging mattress no longer seemed charming.

We can assume here a visceral memory of shitting my pants as a kid, whether or not I was aware of it.

Morning tea and toast in the dark-paneled hotel dining room; John said, "From now on you have to be more careful about what you eat."

My mother's stories about disagreeing with my father were likely to conclude, "I didn't say a word."

Possibly I was ashamed of my inner turmoil, since I mentioned none of it to John.

He and Gabby went to see the Blue Mosque and to find me some Pepto-Bismol.

I shit the tea and toast away.

I lay in my hammock-like bed staring at the cracked ceiling, muttering "Fuck, fuck, fuck!" at each new twist of my gut.

Wanting the diarrhea to pass was the same as wanting the doubt and confusion to pass.

As my thoughts escalated into a kind of falsetto, I began to debate whether to break up with John right there in Cairo.

Preemptive abandonment.

Yet I was also running away from my own roiling suppositions and imperatives.

It would have been a lot simpler to see a doctor, but in the mental maze I'd entered, a parasite must have seemed the least of my problems.

I wondered if there was such a thing as Egyptian saltine crackers.

I felt no better the next day and desperately tried to decide whether I was too sick to travel to Aswan that night, as John and I had planned. I couldn't stay in Cairo alone—should I go to back to Israel with Gabby?

Lying there fervently wishing John would proclaim to me, "I'll come with you to Israel and make sure you get well!"

John said we had already bought our tickets to Aswan and moreover he didn't know when he would ever get back to Egypt, so he definitely wanted to go to Aswan.

This wasn't particularly considerate of him, but I'm concerned here with my own actions.

I thought, "My boyfriend is selfish and won't take care of me!"

It might have been interesting to conduct this conversation out loud, but even on a good day, I couldn't have conceived of a happy result.

I've since learned that John responds well to direct requests, but I had little inkling of this then.

On the other hand I was also sure I would be better soon, as I always had been whenever I had caught a stomach bug up until now.

In the end I agreed to go with John up the Nile, but even at the train station I considered turning back.

I climbed onto the top bunk of our compartment and began to shiver uncontrollably—a fresh symptom.

The carriage shuddered and began to roll.

John asked the steward for an extra blanket, but its warmth had no effect.

The guidebook warned of fundamentalist rebels shooting at these trains; I imagined the black window strafed by bullets.

Click-clack, click-clack.

Weak and sweating through my clothes, almost beyond thought now—except for the conviction that getting on this train with John had been the biggest mistake of my life.

7

JOHN SAID, "LOOK," and I sat up to behold in the window of our compartment the hazy gardens of the Nile, plots of the purest green and rows of spindly trees, filing slowly past in the ancient early morning light. "Wow," I said. My fever had broken. In the next field a slender figure in a white turban and pale blue robe, his back to us, glided calmly between the calmly glowing furrows. Now and then we caught a glimpse of the river and the sandy banks on the other side. It was as if the train had traveled backward in time while I slept, and even now was crawling still further into previous eras, slowed by the effort. The landscape before us had nothing to do with the train or anything else invented in the past five thousand years. John and I were invisible, gazing out like spirits on an untouched world.

8

THE HOTEL IN ASWAN was a rundown sixties high-rise of chipped pink stucco, with cracked balconies overlooking debris-strewn lots.

We were on the far edge of town on the far edge of Egypt.

It was hard to find anything I could eat.

Locating a decent doctor here seemed even more out of the question than in Cairo.

We had prepaid for the room, and it felt too extravagant to move to a better hotel where, say, toast and tea might be served.

John went out to explore the city, returning at lunchtime to tell of dark-skinned men offering him "Nubian banana" on the *corniche*.

"It's definitely more like Africa here," John said, entranced.

Indeed he had been entranced ever since we stepped off the plane, as if Egypt were his ideal hallucinogen.

I spent the afternoon alone in the hot room—sleeping, sweating, writing in my journal, going to the balcony now and then.

Distant palm trees, the sliver of a sailboat on the shimmering water—the very felucca John was on?

"Like a wheel of fortune," sang my Walkman, "I heard my fate turn, turn, turn."

Memory of overhearing my mother say to my father, "Why can't you do something nice for me, like taking me out to dinner, without my having to ask you?" I was six or seven. The fact that I remember the exchange is evidence of how rarely she stuck up for herself like that.

Here the desert went right up to the Nile's banks.

Memory of her blood in the toilet bowl.

"I want to run away," I wrote, "not only from here but from all of my life."

Memory of helping G. pick out a new bed and, after we had brought it to his apartment, his declaring it was presumptuous for me to assume we'd spend the night together. "I feel invaded," he said.

"A warm knife in my belly," I wrote, "another in my head."

Tourists were advised to take a taxi convoy to the temple of Edfu, because a single car was subject to rebel attack, but in any case I doubted I would be well enough to go.

I stared longingly at the guidebook's photo of Edfu.

I began debating again whether to break up with John.

I was hoping for some kind of self-help rule, a clear line marking when you should or shouldn't leave someone.

Living under full sway of my illusions will forever be one sense of the word "Egypt" for me.

Perhaps America could say the same thing of "Islam."

"I seem destined to see little more than this crappy hotel room."

If, say, during lunch I had stopped to observe even for one moment John's wide face and green brown eyes, I might have brought myself to my senses, at least a little.

For a minute I thought maybe I was feeling a little better.

It was very hot and I could muster walking for less than fifteen minutes before stopping to rest on a bench overlooking the Nile.

I had never seen a sunset like this: lacy rags in clumps, connected by ropes of cumulus, sometimes the ropes crossing at right angles, all of this in a single plane high above the Nile, above sand hills, like an orchestra of ragged clouds, rows of gray, dark gold, bright gold, all arranged around the conductor of the sun—

A man in a long blue kaftan stood in front of me—"Smoke, smoke. I take care of you."

I moved to another bench.

I'm not usually one to see pictures in the sky.

Four cassocks seemed to be dancing wildly off to one side, their hands linked, and soon they were spun apart by their own dancing.

As it turned out, I was much better the following day, in both mind and body, and in Luxor John and I went out to see the gigantic pillars of Karnak; a cramped tomb painted above with grape vines; the vast temple of Queen Hatshepsut cut into the hillside, where fifty-eight tourists and four Egyptians would be knifed or gunned down by rebels only a month later . . .

John and I did go back into couples therapy, but not until five years later.

For now, I continued sitting by the Nile, gazing into the sunset, re-asking myself all the riddles of the day.

And then there it was, a parting in the clouds in the shape of a question mark, blurry but unmistakable, with even a small blue chink below for the dot.

I stared at it in thwarted wonder, until new shapes appeared —a plus, a circle.

I stumbled back to the hotel to wait for my boyfriend.

SUNNY VIEW

1

ALONG THE DRY pinkish hills I drove west on the Interstate toward the white brown hazy flatness below, where my eighty-eight-year-old mother lay in a hospital bed.

She had broken her hip just outside my parents' hotel room in Yosemite and had been taken by ambulance first to the closest hospital and then to a larger hospital in Modesto for surgery.

My siblings were all on their way to Santiago, for my nephew's wedding.

I'm not describing a dream: the wedding really was in Santiago.

My mother's illness had jolted me out of my usual joys and problems, just as it now jolts this narrative out of the past.

I wasn't speeding but had with all good speed bought a one way airline ticket, booked the car reservation, mapped my route from the airport, woken early, climbed into the radio cab to JFK, boarded the plane, exited the plane, rented the SUV, and gotten on the road, all in less than twenty-four hours, hoping that each step would bring me closer to everything turning out okay.

Until now (October 2003) my parents had never been seriously ill.

Though I could see nothing of the vast smoggy valley below, I liked sitting up so high in the SUV.

If there was news of Iraq on the radio, I wasn't listening.

My parents hadn't told us about the accident until after my mother's surgery, two days later.

"Hang on for Mom," said Dad, and her weak, clogged voice came on the line.

Notes on the back of my journal:

> surgery "successful"—plates and screws—yesterday
> —started physical therapy today
> —stay in a facility in San Jose 3 weeks—"skilled nursing facility"

To Do List: Save Mom.

Down in the Central Valley I merged onto an older highway and after twenty minutes or so looped around onto one of those glary California boulevards of dingy stucco apartment complexes, telephone wires, huge fast food signs, and empty treeless sidewalks.

The haziness of San Jose was nothing compared to the haziness of Modesto.

The Vagabond Motel, where my father was staying, consisted of several two-story wooden structures lined with identical blue doors and floor-length aluminum windows.

Outside the lobby I ran into the Hendersons, the couple from my parents' church who that morning had generously driven up from San Jose, but almost before I could thank them Mrs. Henderson exclaimed, "When we got here we found David [my father] just *wandering* around the motel—he couldn't find his *room*, and we had to *take* him there."

I stammered, as if in my father's defense, "He's probably very upset."

To say that I myself was upset just then would place too neat a label on an amorphous array of emotions regarding an already scary state of affairs whose complexities had now apparently multiplied to include the total failure of my father's memory.

Mrs. Henderson reiterated that my father didn't know where he was and that I would need to watch him carefully—meaning, I assumed, that I had fallen down on the job so far.

Indeed, my siblings and I had been ignoring his increasing senility for years.

I might have expected the Hendersons to accompany me to the hospital or at least to my father's motel room, but they made it clear they weren't staying a moment longer in Modesto, now that I—the Family Member—had arrived.

Possibly I'm being unfair. I've found that life and death situations heighten my sense of both gratitude and indignation.

I asked the desk clerk for a room next to my father's.

Outside the lobby, three separate palms in a bed of lava rocks.

2

ONE SATURDAY NIGHT when I was eleven, there was nothing good on TV and we came upon a black and white movie that Mom said must have been an old serial—one cliffhanger after another, including the heroine literally hanging off a cliff— and Mom could barely contain her laughter.

She loved unintended humor.

Another time when there was nothing good on, my oldest brother, Paul, suggested we turn down the sound and put on a record; just as someone died on a submarine, the Beatles sang, "Your mother should know."

My own mother laughed and laughed.

She was remarkably open to such experiments, which I gather Paul and his college friends had conducted while stoned.

I mention these stray happy memories to counterbalance what follows.

In the hospital my mother said, "Dad didn't want to call you kids, but I said we had to. He can't drive. He can't go look at nursing homes for me. He can't see well enough now even to cook for himself a can of soup."

He must have been standing right beside me, but he had always blithely ignored my mother's criticisms.

I don't recall his reaction when I had first arrived at his motel room; possibly he put on a brave face; possibly he was simply numb; I don't remember him seeming nearly as addled as the Hendersons had described, but of course I was now on hand to provide the necessary hints.

My mother explained that only part of her hip had been replaced, which meant an easier rehab than for a full hip replacement.

The thin colorless hospital gown didn't cover her well; her chest looked exposed and pale with its dark moles and purplish spots; and her hair was a lopsided clump of gray.

I had never seen her look so terrible and I feared for her life.

At the other end of the ward, the hospital social worker offered me her list of three nursing homes in San Jose that had room for my mother.

Rehabilitation would take several weeks. Medicare would pay for nursing care and for physical therapy but not for the ambulance to San Jose, nor for any sort of care beyond the prescribed period of rehab, though my mother would probably still require assistance when she returned home.

I tried to take in these simple facts but as I sat in the social worker's small office, staring at her stacks of colored forms, it all seemed immensely confusing and complex, as if I had just arrived in a foreign land.

I asked whether my mother might go to the retirement community near San Jose where my parents were already on the waiting list, and the social worker said she could arrange that if Sunny View had a bed available in their nursing facility. The next step, she said, was for me to go look at Sunny View and the other homes on the list in order to make a selection. I didn't think to ask what my criteria should be.

Back in my mother's room: the IV taped to her thin, blue wrist, and my father saying, "I know, dear . . ."

3

THE VAGABOND'S SLICK polyester bedspreads, rust, gold, and green in a "patchwork" pattern, and the cheap white quilting when the spread was turned back.

On my Walkman, Blue Nile's Paul Buchanan, in his Scottish brogue: "I'm tired of crying on the stairs!"

Vague memory of my father and me having dinner together in a Denny's-like restaurant and, in the morning, eating free doughnuts in the motel lobby before going to the hospital again.

Fortunately it seemed like a good hospital.

My mother didn't want us to stay long; she was anxious for me to get down to San Jose and get cracking.

Objective statement: She couldn't seem to hold in her head both her good and bad feelings toward my father, so she had to vent the bad ones onto some third party, such as her friends or her children.

"If we were already at Sunny View, then all this would be taken care of," she said now, meaning that if my father had not resisted moving to the retirement community when an apartment the right size had become available two years earlier, we would not have to find a nursing facility now, nor would I have to look after my father while she was recovering.

The deterioration of her hearing in recent years seemed to have bolstered her fiction that my father could not hear her complaints about him, even if he was two feet away.

At some point, either in the hospital or later, she complained of his bungling the call to the front desk at the Ahwahnee Hotel in Yosemite, to alert them of her fall.

He hadn't been able to see the numbers on the phone in the room.

"I said, 'Just dial zero! The bottom key!' But he's never been good in a crisis."

My brain rushed first to save her from him, then him from her.

Noelle, my therapist, later referred to this as "sequential mistrust."

The old sensation of being ripped in two, but I'm thick cardboard and hard to rip, so I'm mostly being twisted this way and that.

I'm like my mother that way—weirdly strong.

4

APHORISM: HAVING TO choose between your parents as a kid leads to crippling inner turmoil as an adult.

Panicky belief that I had to take drastic action to protect myself from anything I didn't like about John, hence I continued the practice of leaving him in my mind, though not with the same intensity as in Egypt.

I still also preferred imaginary arguments to actual ones.

A year earlier we had begun seeing a couples therapist, Armin, in order to address just such problems.

We had nearly broken up.

Mainly we were trying to learn how to have an honest disagreement, a simple enough concept in theory.

I, for one, had not yet weaned myself from needing a referee, Armin, in order to speak my mind.

And then there was my nasty tendency to blame John for things we both had done or decided.

Sample entry from my journal that fall: "Yesterday Noelle and I reached the same point again—my ambivalence won't protect me; being half-committed to John won't keep me safe—I need to fully commit and see what happens."

Part of me would like to tell you more about couples therapy, and part of me knows it has to remain between John and me.

5

IN THE CAR, on the same hazy Interstate going west back through the grassy hillsides, just as we crested a very long grade, my father broke down crying.

"I don't want Mom to die," he said.

He was ninety and I was forty-six and I had never seen him this way.

I thought:
1. This is the last thing I need right now.
2. He's no good in a crisis.
3. I need to take care of my mother!

The pink hills dotted by black live oaks, the dirty too-bright sky, and the raised lane markers ticking past the SUV's shiny white fenders.

A concept in couples therapy that I was still trying to grasp was what Armin called "Detach With Love." It had something to do with seeing myself as distinct from John, with my own opinion, yet still connected to him.

Now, in some minor miracle of therapeutic training, an unafraid yet receptive state of mind unaccountably took hold of me, allowing me to glance over at my father and simply see him there, crying in the seat next to me.

Here the reader might expect a physical description of him, but the only picture that comes to mind is that of his limp hands in his lap and the blank haze outside his window. In fact, I may not even have glanced over at him, since I was driving, or because I was afraid to look too closely, and anyway what I saw at that moment wasn't physical.

I thought:
     1. Does his crying stop me from what I need to do today?
     2. What if I simply let my father cry?
     3. In fact, I *want* a father who can cry.

And in this way, I was able to say to him, simply, "I know, Dad," and to reach out and pat his shoulder.

The process took perhaps ten seconds, from his outburst to my freaking out to my comforting him, and I had kept one hand on the steering wheel the whole time.

I hadn't even changed lanes.

Already my father's sobs were subsiding and I understood that he had required from me a surprisingly small amount of kindness.

6

I WANT THOSE ten seconds to last forever so my life could always be that calm and revelatory, but now I must describe the rest of my stay in California.

I imagine my father began to cry because at the crest of that hill he fully realized we were returning to San Jose without my mother, which is exactly what he feared might happen in a bigger way.

There may have been a previous outburst at the motel or the hospital, and I ignored it, or maybe he had tried to be strong until now.

My father and I were silent for several minutes as I continued driving down the gray pebbly freeway, which was now descending through the arid hills into the Bay Area.

In a show of mental competence, he told me exactly where to turn off the Interstate in San Jose, then off the expressway, off the avenue, and onto our own street, Del Cambre Drive.

The old familiar house, now motherless, where I fixed lunch in the old familiar kitchen.

The reassuring metal click as each cabinet door clutched the magnet.

In an older part of town we found the first facility on our list, clearly the cheapest, and though I expected soul-stealing dreariness, a small white dog barked as we walked in, making the hospital-green walls seem almost cheerful.

I had no idea what questions to ask but tried things like, "How often does the doctor visit?" and "Is there always an RN on duty?"

Spanish wafting from a room nearby signaled the home's working-class status, and I doubted my mother would like it here.

At the next home, in a swankier part of the valley, the rotund male administrator implored me to send my mom here for rehab, because this facility, unlike some, was tirelessly dedicated to getting patients back on their feet, and this was exactly what she needed, not a conventional nursing home where people tend to languish.

There must be a specific area of the limbic system that lights up during such emergencies—PARENT IN TROUBLE— and this area had been blinking in my line of vision for two solid days now, hence for the moment I allowed myself the luxury of feeling taken under this nice man's wing.

Back in the car I decided he had come on too strong, though in retrospect I think he may have been right, who knows.

Between nursing homes, the usual freeways of San Jose, the familiar trees in brownish sunlight, and the expected pale mountains on the horizon, blue to the west, pink to the east.

Up in the foothills the most expensive home displayed everywhere its Hyatt Regency level furniture and wallpaper.

Near a pastel sitting area I beheld a row of ten or twelve very old people slumped in their wheelchairs, completely out of it, one or two of them softly moaning, and no nurse in sight.

I crossed this home off the list.

The road to Sunny View went straight down a long steep hill and back up another equally long steep hill; the facility stood at the top of that second incline, though in fact it had no view.

The middle-aged saleslady with her dyed reddish hair and small beauty-contestant nose struck me as a perfect cross between a funeral director and real estate agent, and the décor of her windowless office achieved the same curious balance, with its dark green walls and heavy traditional furniture also in dark hues.

She made sure to look at my father as she spoke: Yes, Sunny View could offer Ruth a room in its nursing wing, and as it happened, a very nice, large apartment was opening up soon in Assisted Living, where both of them could live after Ruth had recovered.

She led us down several long white corridors to Nursing, where the RN gave the usual assurances.

There were a couple of moaners somewhere down a hallway, out of sight, but there was a patio and a small garden; overall the mood wasn't as grim as the expensive home we had just seen, nor as cheerful as the facility with the barking dog; similarly, the sales pitch fell somewhere in the middle in terms of helpful information versus playing on our emotions; hence, in some kind of Goldilocks logic, and because I had no other logic to go by, Sunny View felt about right.

7

I ADMIT THAT my various acts of elder care included an unspoken message: "This is what I wanted from you—empathy, time, assistance—that I didn't always get, either as a child or as an adult."

Kindness as grievance.

After Katrina, my mother said, "Those people should help *themselves.*" That was later, after my father's stroke, but she had always held such views, and my father would have agreed.

The sneaky myth that by being magnanimous to my parents in their old age I could somehow change them, or even that I could change the past—as if adult actions could have a domino effect on childhood.

Trying to transcend my own upbringing, at the scene of the crime.

When I was a kid we lived in Connecticut, Illinois, Louisiana, and two cities in California, all before I was nine.

My siblings and I were more or less banned from mentioning any unhappiness about moving.

I have two memories of Connecticut, which we left when I was a toddler: 1) fear of the upright vacuum cleaner's head-light in the dark living room; 2) learning to pee standing up, from my father.

The move to Illinois proved disastrous—my father lost his new job after just two months.

Evidently my mother hadn't wanted to move there in the first place. The family had lived in Connecticut more than ten years, and my mother was good friends with the next door neighbor, Mrs. Thompson. My mother's amateur symphony in Norwalk, for which she played the violin, had once had Isaac Stern as a soloist.

The oft-repeated tale of basement floods and burst pipes in the new house.

It was in Illinois that my mother's displeasure with my father appears to have become most crippling, a period when I was age three to five.

"*My* yearbooks were ruined, and of course *his* were on a higher shelf."

It's possible I date this as a key period in my parents' marriage only because it was a key period of my own life, but I don't think so.

My father was then in his late forties; he had bought a white Oldsmobile convertible with red interior, which he soon wrecked.

"He lost that job because he talked back to his boss."

There were five children—the oldest two in college, and me not yet in kindergarten. Coming six years after my closest brother, surely I was unplanned, possibly unwanted.

Carol and Helen had to withdraw from their private colleges and attend the University of Illinois instead. I went to nursery school, so my mother could temp in Chicago.

My father found a temporary position with a hairspray manufacturer in another city in Illinois, and when he finally landed a permanent job, with a banana importer in New Orleans, my mother was unable to sell the house; thus for more than a year my parents lived mainly apart.

And so came the moment in the kitchen when I asked myself, "Who is that nice man making popcorn?"

Looking up at him not unkindly, but in genuine confusion.

This would suggest intense loyalty to my mom, and/or intense bereavement for my dad.

As soon as the house was sold, she doggedly packed us up and moved us to a suburb of New Orleans.

I wonder how many more times I'll need to go over this story in my mind.

I looked down from my bedroom window in Louisiana at the mosquito truck going by, kids running after it, possibly on a dare, shouting in the poison fog.

For some reason I remember the uncrating of the dishwasher. It was a portable dishwasher that had to be connected by hoses to the sink.

There in Louisiana, reunited with my father, I forgot I was toilet trained and began shitting my pants.

8

BACK AT THE house Dad agreed that Sunny View was probably the best place for Mom to undergo rehab, but he didn't see why the two of them had to move there permanently: when she was well again, she could simply return to the house.

My mother had severe osteoporosis, and I've never seen anyone more bent over.

"We have everything we need right here," my father said, with his old complacency.

Indeed as usual a cool jasmine-scented breeze was wafting through the dining room window, and the oranges were glowing out on the tree in the backyard.

Perhaps I said Mom could no longer be expected to take care of the house, or perhaps I didn't want to upset him.

Over ice cream he exclaimed what a good job I had done that day.

I intuited an element of flattery—perhaps to get me on his side regarding the Sunny View question—but his praise also seemed genuine.

I had often heard him praise my mother in just this way.

That night at my old desk I jotted down the pros and cons of each nursing facility, so that I could present them to my mother back in Modesto, the next morning.

I lay on my old bed as Eno's accordion-like keyboard glided through Baroque-like chords.

The morning paper dutifully reported, "Teams in Iraq on Trail of Anthrax and Missiles, Chief Searcher Says."

My father and I drove the various roads and freeways.

When we got there my mother was tired from physical therapy but her color was good.

I wanted her to feel like she had a choice, and I wanted the same for my father, so I very carefully said, "*If* you and Dad decide to move to Sunny View, then you'll already be there."

She shrugged and chose Sunny View.

9

AT LEAST ONCE a day my father said he wished his vision were better, and he couldn't have done any of this without me.

I myself was surprised at how well I handled a situation that was unlike anything I'd encountered before, since I hadn't been directly involved in Ken's care.

I returned the rented SUV and rode the bus back, which took two and a half hours, and began driving my mother's car; I went to Sunny View to wait for my mother's ambulance from Modesto but she had already arrived and was asleep; I asked Mrs. Henderson to ask her daughter the doctor for the name of a good orthopedist; I brought Mom's hospital X-rays from Sunny View to the orthopedist's office; I went with Dad to shop for a walker for Mom; I gathered the clothes she had requested from her closet as well as a brush for her hair; I called the hotel at Yosemite to see if her right hearing aid had perhaps been found; I located her old right hearing aid in exactly the dresser drawer where she had told me I would find it; I went to buy warm socks for her, because she said her feet had been cold in the hospital.

Dad and I visited Mom every day, usually once in the morning and once in the afternoon, which I hoped the staff would notice and thus pay closer attention to her.

Regarding Dad's reluctance to move out of the house: "He just isn't being realistic."

"Sure, you can hire homecare workers, but then who oversees the homecare workers?"

"And how would I even get down into the family room, with a walker?"

Always speaking to me, as if Dad weren't there.

"I don't think you get much for your money at Sunny View," he replied.

His argument wasn't new, but his hearing was excellent.

From my journal: "I've had to encourage them both; their apparent inability to encourage each other has baffled me."

Panicky swims at the Y and panicky walks past my old schoolyard, around the track, out the other side, past more tract homes.

My love and my anger, in a tight, tight ball.

Confiding with John each night after dinner, the curly phone cord pulled out into the garage, wondering if Dad could still hear me, just like I used to do in high school.

Talking to Noelle on Mom's cell phone, sitting on the bleachers of the empty Little League diamond.

"When two people have been together as long as your parents have," said Noelle, "they're like one person. So when you calm one of them down, you calm them both down."

She was reassuring me that my efforts weren't actually split.

The row of pastel 1960s houses backing up on the dirt and weedy edge of the baseball fields.

My mother had been a bookkeeper much of her life and often used to tell stories of searching for a missing penny when the various columns didn't add up.

Ironically, my father admired her perfectionism. "Mom does everything perfectly," he liked to say.

She was annoyed that the nurse's aides often missed doses of her glaucoma medication, but she wasn't allowed to administer the drops herself.

"I keep telling them, I AM DIABETIC, and they keep trying to give me APPLE SAUCE."

Most of the nurse's aides spoke highly accented English, and even my mother's one good hearing aid didn't work very well.

One night the aide made my mother wait for more than an hour in a wet diaper. "You know, you're not the only patient here," the aide told her.

I complained, but a few days later it happened again.

Journal: "I don't know if I should be taking better care of her, but I also know she's rather particular . . . she gets mad that the nurse's aide opens the wrong side of the little milk carton."

I bought a mindfulness meditation tape and began listening to it twice a day.

"You will merely make a mental note of whatever enters your awareness, at the moment you become aware of it . . . If next you thought about your mother, you would say, 'Now I am thinking about my mother.'"

The usual daily naps and masturbation.

I listened to each of her complaints, making sympathetic nods, trying to decide which ones were worth passing along to the RN and which were not.

Fake violins plucking: "My brain is a chemical factory, capable of producing any necessary chemical to ensure my being a stress-free person."

Some of Sunny View's wheelchairs were more comfortable than others, with various kinds of seats, and only some of them had footrests, which the physical therapist said my mother needed, and just when we had found her a good one, the staff would take all the wheelchairs outside to be washed, and the same one never seemed to come back to her.

The additional cushions my mother required would also be washed, and she would often end up with an unsuitable one.

I complained but was told the wheelchair-washing procedure could not be altered.

Possibly I should have been more forceful with Sunny View about such things.

My abhorrence of conflict makes me a sympathetic friend and interviewer, but leaves a lot of unsolved problems lying around.

Such as with John.

Whenever I'm forced to confront someone, my face heats up immediately and my head floods with an indescribable prickly sensation akin to a fever dream I once had in which my sheets were immense boulders.

My parents' longtime doctor was semi-retired and would not visit Mom at Sunny View—nor would the orthopedist, of course—and getting her out of the wheelchair, into the car, out of the car, into the wheelchair, and into the doctor's office was an ordeal through which she repeatedly winced and groaned in both annoyance and pain.

Journal: "It's all so emotional and so *logistical* at the same time."

In Nursing she was surrounded by patients who were completely senile, and sometimes the staff treated her like a child.

She imitated the saccharine voice of a volunteer: "'Would you like to come sing a song with us, dear?'" Then she wheeled me in *there*, and I had to *sit* while they all sang 'Yes, Jesus Loves Me.'"

She had to do various exercises in bed, such as lift herself up with the help of a bar that hung from the ceiling, and one time as she completed this movement she called out to the physical therapist, "Blast off!"

Quips such as this as well as her determination endeared my mother to this therapist, a young heavy-set woman, possibly a dyke, one of the few at Sunny View who actually seemed to know what she was doing.

Dad and I came in one day to see Mom walking very slowly in the hallway, with great concentration, her veiny hands tightly gripping the walker as its rubber wheels slowly turned on the pale institutional tile.

I said, "You're walking!" and she replied simply, "Yes," still concentrating very hard on placing each sneaker a few inches ahead at a time.

I doubted my father would have had the will to come back from such an injury.

Her death just two and a half years later makes palpable the mystery of that effort: it wasn't exactly futile, but what exactly was it?

Tiny and bent over and moving her feet under the awful fluorescent lighting.

10

"OPEN UP EVERY cell of your body to light and love."

The warm feeling of cooking for my dad, of choosing foods I knew he was accustomed to, such as sliced ham from the supermarket, reheated in the microwave.

Difficult to see him objectively, since to consider his faults is to enter into my mother's system again.

The familiar loud sluicing of the dishwasher.

The lumpy ceramic tiles of the entry hall, across which the hard plastic wheels of Mom's laundry cart used to clack.

I put drops in Dad's small blue eyes each night, because he couldn't manage it himself.

"You are a remarkably competent person," he said. "Thanks, Dad," I replied, half-realizing that up till now he had thought of me as a loser.

"Why don't you write a bestseller?" he used to ask me.

In contrast, my mother had always been proud of my writing, even when I published unflattering accounts of her and my father. She went to see me read from my first book, *The Hurry-Up Song*, which is no more upbeat about my family than is this memoir; my father, however, stayed home.

Regarding my longstanding job at the magazine, he said now, "They must like you," because my boss had told me to take as much time off as I needed to care for my parents.

We went to buy his cherry Life Savers in bulk.

My father had always asked lots of questions, which I had found aggressive—"the third degree," my mother called it— and maybe we were right, but presumably he was also curious.

"Don't you get lonely, living by yourself?" he asked now, sounding very concerned. We were on the way back from Smart & Final. I replied that I saw John on weekends and often went out with friends on weeknights.

While my mother had been forthcoming in her acceptance of my being gay, until now my father had never said anything about it at all.

Another day, over lunch, I was recalling a camping vacation John and I had taken to Joshua Tree and Death Valley, how we ended the trip on a beach down near San Luis Obispo, pitching our tent in view of the ocean, which we could hear all night.

Suddenly Dad said, 'So John is like your wife?"
    I was about to take my usual umbrage with him but then decided he was simply speaking his own language.
    "Yes," I said, "I suppose John *is* like my wife."

I don't mean to idealize my father here, who in order to keep peace with my mother had allowed her to gripe about him to her kids all those years.

Her complaining and his complacency: add love, for there was indeed love between them, and you have my original definition of marriage.

Later in the week Dad re-expressed his concern that I wasn't married, as if we had never had that conversation about John-as-wife.

He may have forgotten it completely, or maybe he remembered later, forgot again, remembered again . . .

Sunny View's deadline to accept the apartment in Assisted Living was approaching.

My mother's friends Hap and Mary had each expressed to me their opinion that, for my mother's sake, my parents had to sell their house and move into the apartment.

Hap herself already lived at Sunny View, because her husband could no longer walk.

Dad playing solitaire on his old green blotter, under the bright, bright fluorescent desk lamp.

I must have been reading some book, but I have no memory of what.

The fake wood wainscoting, installed because our old dog Sam had clawed the wallpaper.

Familiar shapes in the rough stucco walls of my old room, such as a pig with a long snout.

Mary had also tried to persuade me to go to church with her. I declined. She looked crestfallen.

Though I agreed with my mother about Sunny View, in fairness to my father I set up a meeting at the house with a guy from a homecare company. He was very blow-dried, very sales-y, and he gave us an attractive brochure. The high cost didn't seem to deter my father.

I set up a second meeting, at Sunny View, with my mother. "As I've said *many times*, I don't *want* homecare," she said.

Out in the hallway, the salesman said, "I don't recommend homecare for Mrs. Chase."

On the phone my sister Carol agreed it was wisest for me to stay out of the argument as much as possible, but I refrained from taking sides in a fog—just as I would have *taken* sides in a fog.

11

ONE AFTERNOON MOM began talking about death. It wasn't that there were no secrets between us now but there were fewer secrets because I had seen her "this way" every day for more than two weeks—her thin hospital gown, her matted hair, her irritability, and her determination to recover. I don't recall where Dad was during this particular visit. Possibly home napping. I don't think I had gone there to talk to Mom about Sunny View without him, since that would have felt conspiratorial and I was trying so hard not to conspire. She told me that back in the hospital in Modesto she had thought she might die, because that's how it used to be: a broken hip meant the end. But she hadn't been afraid of dying, she said. And just as she would do in a dream I had after she died, she told me she knew there really was no such thing as death; rather, she would simply go "someplace else." And I replied, just as I would in the dream, that "basically I believe that too." The dream version of the conversation concluded there, but the real conversation continued. It was then that she told me, for the first time in my life, that she had nearly died when I was born. "I never knew that," I murmured. I had known only that the labor was long, and in the end I was born Caesarean. Now she told me that during the operation she had floated up above the table and looked down at the

175

doctors and nurses working on her. "The next thing I remember," she said, "I was waking up in the recovery room. In a little while the doctor came in. I didn't mention what had happened, but he said to me, 'You must live right.' That's all he said. So I knew I hadn't just dreamt it or something. And since then, I haven't been afraid of dying." Given all the things she had revealed to me in my life that she shouldn't have, it seems a miracle of willpower that she had never revealed this until now. Presumably she felt the information might make me feel unwanted, or set apart from the other kids, or extra beholden to her, all of which was indeed how I felt now—like there was a mystical bond between us, and I was responsible for her.

12

PART OF ME welcomes the information about my birth and part of me finds it troubling.

She revealed this to me the day before she and my father had to decide whether or not to move to Sunny View.

At the time I accepted the revelation as simply a logical extension of the topic "I Thought I Might Die," and I felt curiously privileged to be let in on a long-held secret of which I myself was the very crux.

Inevitably the story had the effect on me of "final words."

It had always been Dad who spoke of the phenomenon of near-death experiences, an interest that had seemed merely eccentric, but now I understood his reasons.

The revelation added yet another layer of fog as I continued trying to do what I thought was best for both of my parents.

Wanting to be Mom's special one, the one who could protect her, yet not wanting it.

May the white space here represent the small distance I sought to place between her and myself. And still seek.

A layer of air around her.

As in a novel my memory skips seamlessly to the next morning, which suggests to me a night of mindless inner turmoil like heavy sludge.

"As you breathe in, feel yourself breathing in love."

Dad and I ate our breakfast as usual and then headed over to Sunny View, also as usual.

Down the long hill and back up again.

I was afraid Dad would dig in his heels and then I really would have to take my mother's side.

The dry sun-drenched live oaks in Sunny View's parking lot, their waxy prickly leaves in harsh October sunlight.

At some point I had realized that, with novelistic concision, the nursing home where I had worked in high school as a dishwasher was none other than Sunny View itself; the facility's many new buildings had, at first, obscured this fact.

I used to find dentures on the food trays.

An aide once told me that an old man cried when informed there were no more bananas that day.

At the moment I had no use for such memories, which had always made me think of nursing homes as "gross and depressing," whereas now I needed to regard them as "not so bad after all."

Dad and I passed through the lobby with its particular smell.

I wheeled Mom out into the small garden, and the three of us were sitting in the deep blue shade.

A general atmosphere of California flowery fragrance.

I might have left my parents alone to have it out, but I didn't think that was wise, though in choosing to preside over their argument I was perhaps indulging my longstanding myth that I was somehow in charge of their marriage.

Once again Dad said, "I just don't think you get much for your money at a retirement home," and, "We have everything we need at the house."

"*He* has everything *he* needs," Mom replied. "Because *I* do *everything!*"

This was quite true: she handled all the finances as well as the cooking and cleaning, and of course now the driving too.

I knit my brow: if ever there was a time to take Mom's side, this might be it.

In couples therapy, whenever John or I tried to talk to each other through Armin, he (Armin) would say to John or me, "Tell him, not me. He's sitting right here."

Thus I found myself saying to my mother now, "Tell him, not me. He's sitting right here."

I wish I could see the humor in this—serving as couples counselor to my own parents.

"David, I just can't do it anymore," my mother croaked, as annoyed at me now as she was at my father. "I'm *tired*. I *cannot* cook and clean anymore. I don't have the strength in my legs to drive, so how would we even get to the supermarket? And I *cannot* hire someone and try to oversee them. It *just won't work.*"

Fighting for herself from a wheelchair.

The temperature must have been about eighty; otherwise it would have been either too cold or too hot for her to be out in the garden.

She made various other statements to which I said, "Tell Dad, not me."

Above, the sky was that utterly cloudless California blue.

A couple of times I let her speak to me without making her repeat it to my father, such as when she listed all the services that Sunny View would provide.

"There are meals. And housekeeping. And I'm going to need help with bathing and going to the bathroom and getting dressed in the morning!"

"I know that, Ruth," my father admitted.

"And who is going to put in your eye drops? I can barely put my own socks on."

Confronted directly with my mother's arguments, my father appeared increasingly stricken and defeated.

His almost white hair and his thin white short-sleeve polyester shirt.

He had probably sensed my real position on Sunny View, so I felt like a traitor anyway.

Nearby, cherry tomatoes glowed. The beds were raised waist high, so that residents in wheelchairs could tend them.

At last my father said, "All right, Ruth."

No memory of his expression, but let's say he was staring down at the cracked concrete, his hands flat on his knees.

I waited a moment. "So you're going to take the apartment?" I asked.

"Yes," he replied.

"All right then," said my mother, angrily.

Fatigue had been accruing like a pair of heavy goggles around my eye sockets ever since my arrival in California, and now I wanted to curl up in a ball right on the patio.

Thus concluded my heroic self-help project to remain neutral in my parents' dispute and thus forge a new relationship to both of them before it was too late.

My mother liked to call me a "caring" person (as opposed to certain other uncaring people she knew), and though I had hoped today to redefine the very term, I now felt conflicted rather than caring.

As much as I hoped for her to get well and as much as I tried to be the best son I could be in the situation and as much as I sympathized with her and as much as I gave her my sympathy and encouragement and as much as I might have even gone overboard with a desire to serve during her time of need, still there was this one thing I wouldn't do for her.

To her mind, my not taking sides was the same as taking my father's side. Paradoxically, if she hadn't always pitted me against him, I might have been able to serve as her advocate that morning at Sunny View.

As it happened, I sort of got my father back, during those three weeks in California.

Evidently the only way for that to happen was with my mother completely out of the house. She had always managed to keep us apart, even as she made such statements as, "You should try to spend more time with Dad."

Recently Noelle said, "She considered you a gift, and she wanted to keep you for herself, but she didn't realize that that also meant keeping your father from *you.*"

The horrible dilemma that put me in, and still puts me in.

Mom versus Dad: having to choose between myself and myself.

Though John and I have gotten better at disagreeing, whenever we do, still some part of me feels hopeless and trapped.

Usually when you read about people who have had near-death experiences, they decide to make big changes in their lives, but evidently my mother made no big changes after floating above the operating table of my birth.

Like most depressed people I'm idealistic, hence often disappointed.

Periodically I return to the exasperated question, "Why did she *do* that?" Not only the complaining about my father, but her needing to put me in the middle of it, no matter how often I protested.

She often said Dad was unrealistic, which was true, but she herself was unrealistic to think she could live that way.

I wonder if it will ever be simple for me to tell John when I'm pissed.

I wonder if I'll ever be objective about my mother.

Then again, why would I want to be?

At some point I gleaned that her friends Hap and Mary thought I hadn't sufficiently stuck up for her against my father.

She must have complained to them.

Periodically I argue with Hap and Mary, in my mind.

THE CONDITION OF
LEFTOVER BAGGAGE

1

THE PLASTIC SHOPPING bag was white with gold letters that advertised, in English, a shoe store in Tehran. I discovered this in my suitcase upon returning to New York from Berlin in October 2006.

I had not, as one must assert at the airport, allowed anyone else to pack for me, nor had I left my luggage unattended.

What happens beyond your ken, as when the shells in the game are moving too quickly to see.

I didn't even know anyone from Iran.

Smashed between the two halves of my suitcase, the shopping bag was stuffed full.

I pulled from it the following items: several children's costumes in bright colors, with gold and silver rickrack; a red woman's dress with a gold scimitar pin; and several books of music for an instrument called the setar, which an illustration showed to be some kind of lute.

I half wondered if this was someone's idea of a joke.

As if the luggage fairy had left me a gift.

Unpacking the suitcase, I couldn't be entirely sure if any of my own things were missing, but I didn't think so.

My bag had been delayed on my flight home, so its return to me intact was—objectively speaking—a relief.

I was in that jetlag state of unreality anyway, where you don't quite know where you are.

I pondered our crack anti-terrorism forces, here or in Europe, randomly inserting random items into random suitcases.

Searching, and mixing things up, with their white-gloved hands.

My mother had died early that year, my father the year before.

I had put aside my grief in order to function on my trip to Holland and Germany, but now I was alone in my apartment again.

The pervasiveness of grief, whether or not you recognize it, like the white on this page.

I began to wonder how the Iranian family must have felt when they realized these particular belongings were missing.

The weird specificity of children's clothing and lute music made me feel as though I had invaded this family's very home.

The costumes' synthetic fabric was slick and refused to stay folded and stacked.

I pictured other indignities suffered by this family upon entering the United States in addition to lost property: intrusive questions, fingerprints, photographs.

Acquaintances in Germany had complained to me about these measures.

And if the contents of the shopping bag had been less innocent, and if I had been "caught" with them?

After Ken died, I constantly misplaced things; now, in some kind of poetic reversal, I had *found* something that wasn't mine.

A small addendum to my inheritance.

Grief, this thing you don't want.

That isn't *yours*.

By now I had more or less accepted my father's death—but my mother's was another story.

The shopping bag's owners appeared to be a mother and her children.

There were no labels on the kids' costumes, so I envisioned the woman sewing them herself—gathering the waists, stitching the rickrack—just as I had seen my mother sew her own clothes and also items for my stuffed bear when I was little.

The music books also evoked my mother, since she had played the violin nearly all her life.

Scales and runs curling from behind the closed door of her study.

The switcheroo: mere memories of a person, subbed in for the person herself.

Had I dreamed about finding music, children's clothing, and a woman's dress in my luggage, I would have concluded that the dream hoped to tell me something about my mother.

In my mind I opened the suitcase again and again, each time finding the white plastic sack that didn't belong there.

*

For all of the above reasons, articulated and unarticulated, I felt compelled to reunite the shopping bag with its rightful owners. I began by calling the airline's number for lost baggage. "Is there a name?" the gruff man asked. "No, I'm sorry, I don't see—" "What are the items?" I began to describe them but of course could not convey their significance to me, which I scarcely understood myself. He interrupted again. "That will be virtually impossible for me to track, sir. A lot of people come through from Iran." I didn't see why these items in particular should be difficult to track. In fact, they could hardly have been more unique. I also doubted that more than a few dozen passengers from Iran arrived in New York on any given day. I had seen a sign for Emirates at the lost-baggage counter when I arrived, so I asked the man if he also handled complaints for that carrier. "Yes, we have an agent dedicated to Emirates," he answered, making no offer to contact this employee. I was becoming exasperated. "Well, do you think the Emirates person might know more?" I asked. There was only the briefest pause, a slight rustling sound. I heard no voices exchanging information. "Nobody has called in reference to any sheet music or children's clothes," he said. "You can either send it back or throw it out."

*

You could say the Iranian shopping bag had good reason to appear in my particular suitcase.

I had been in Europe promoting my novel, *Winkie*, which tells the story of my teddy bear on trial for terrorism.

The idea of Iran as part of an "Axis of Evil" was still relatively recent, and my novel sought to parody such thinking.

I had brought along the bear himself, so that he could appear with me on television.

Surreal to actually see him on TV, the evening following my interview. All in German, of course.

Winkie was then eighty-one years old and very worn out, with a deranged expression resembling Charles Manson.

As in the novel, he had been my mother's teddy bear before he was mine.

With her death, Winkie had become even more precious to me, even more charged than before.

Though I had kept him in my carry-on, somehow he had magnetized my checked baggage for objects as strange and loaded as himself.

While I was writing the book I used to joke to friends that what Winkie most wanted for Christmas was a pink tutu, and indeed the costumes in the shopping bag included a pink satin skirt, short and ruffled.

Winkie's wish had come true.

The novel contains pictures of him in various tiny getups, culminating with a shot of him standing before a backdrop of the pyramids, wearing a blue embroidered tunic and red fez (which I had made out of some felt and a paper cup).

Winkie and the mystery Iranian children—in their bright, gold-trimmed costumes—could almost have been members of the same troupe of performers, a sort of Islamic von Trapp family.

The cover of one of the setar books shows a wooden instrument with a very long, thin neck and bulbous body—a guitar the Cat in the Hat might strum.

I discovered a surprisingly large selection of setar music on iTunes. The tracks I chose sounded vaguely Greek, vaguely Middle Eastern, and at times jangly to my unschooled ears.

My inability to place or enjoy this musical tradition made the tunes seem that much more distant and sad.

The Persian setar is not to be confused with the Indian sitar, says Wikipedia, while an Iranian site describes classical Persian music as "grave and mournful," adding, "The basic character of the Persian is, like his music, melancholy."

*

A few days later I got up the courage to telephone U.S. Customs, realizing I could make my inquiry sound less crazy by calling from my office at the magazine.

Press Officer Jane Rappaport naturally doubted Customs had been responsible for the mix-up but asked me to put my information in an e-mail, including a description of the items I had found.

She called me back the next day. "All I wanted to mention," she said, "is that—let me get my notes—okay." I was heartened that she cared enough both to take notes and to refer to them. She spoke in a raspy Long Island accent that I found disarmingly genuine. She said there were six "leftover" bags from my flight, and if mine was one of them (though she was careful not to confirm this), it would have been inspected by U.S. Customs before it was delivered to me. "We search all luggage that comes in late. There are various threat levels, but you asked if this is because of London"—the bombings that had taken place there two months earlier. "No. We've always had the condition of leftover baggage."

As for the inserted items, she continued, "That could have happened overseas. We have no idea. It wouldn't necessarily have happened here . . . Who knows at what point that piece of luggage was searched, how many clearances it goes through."

Uncertainties seemed to be multiplying.

"You asked also—" she began. "It would be the airline who would help you determine whose stuff that is. We could not identify that for you."

I inquired if my bag might have been searched right alongside other leftover bags that night, causing the mix-up. "Probably not," she said, "because they log in every bag they look at. And if it's cleared, it probably wouldn't be six bags looked at, at the same time."

I didn't find this particularly convincing, but I liked Jane Rappaport herself: she had the appealing oddness of a character actor in a television crime show. Since my e-mail had mentioned the reason for my trip to Europe, I said now, "You know, my novel is about terrorism and childhood, so this is just a really weird coincidence." "Yes!" she exclaimed, and she began singing something, a weird non-tune. It took me a moment to realize it was the theme to *The Twilight Zone*.

2

SEVEN MONTHS EARLIER, the woman at Sunny View had called me at the office. She said my mother had experienced some kind of "event," probably a stroke, and was "unresponsive." I hung up and stared at the white Formica of my desk for a while, before making the necessary calls—the airline; my sisters; John. I got on a plane the next morning. The pilot spoke cheerfully of unusually powerful headwinds, warning us that the flight would take seven or eight hours instead of six. I was in a dazed state of urgency that resembled the heightened concentration demanded by a tragic film. Since I had rushed to California several times for health emergencies during the previous two and a half years, part of me must have thought I was on my way to save her. I could almost feel the wind pushing my body back. The fuselage was my tunnel, softly lit, lined with blue pleather seats, accompanied by the rustling of passengers and the occasional outburst of a toddler. The last time I had seen my mother was at Christmas, two months before. It was not a satisfying visit. She was in nursing care recovering from another fall. My father had died in October, and her main reaction seemed to be renewed anger toward him. If he had let her buy a new recliner a few years ago, then the one in the apartment would not be broken now and we would not have to try to find her a new one when she was too sick to go to a furniture store to make the selection. Complaints of this nature, coming as they did less than three months after my father's death, were almost unbearable to me. I spent as little time with her as possible on that visit, busying myself with the practical details of her care, which were innumerable, and taking long walks in the hills surrounding the retirement home. I regretted this, of course, two months later as the airplane struggled westward. I argued with regretting it—I couldn't have known it would be our last visit, this was just how it had worked out, I had done many nice things for her . . . After three or four hours the pilot came on to say the headwinds were even worse than expected and we would have to stop to refuel in Denver. We lumbered down through the stormy air and slowly landed. We bowled along the pavement to wherever they needed to hook up the hose. I didn't have a window seat and could see only a small space of cold-looking gray. The outsize nature of my frustration prevented me from swearing aloud. I shut my eyes and tried to weep but couldn't. After an unbearably long wait we taxied, waited some more, shuddered up the runway to fly some more against the freakish wind. My brain continued trudging. Is there any point in recalling this? The flight took ten hours in all. In San Jose there was a line of thirty or forty at Hertz, and I waited nearly an hour to reach the counter. I must have read a magazine. By now I was almost reluctant to end the journey. I feared seeing my mother in that state, or seeing her die, or simply facing the fact of her dying. By the time I actually climbed into the rental car, I had become as methodical as my father, a trait that used to drive my mother crazy. I must have still been angry with her, since I'm still angry with her now, as I write this. I went to the hotel to change and to wash my face, reasoning I needed refreshment after pushing through freezing wind for ten hours. I put on a clean shirt. When at last I reached the hospital, late in the afternoon, the nurse said quietly that my mother had died ten minutes earlier.

3

THE SHOE STORE'S phone number is legible on the shopping bag, but I doubted the owners would actually speak English (the shoes are described as "hand maid") and I didn't know anyone who spoke Farsi.

I wasn't even sure if Americans were allowed to call Iran.

John knew a woman who happened to fly one-way the same week as the 9/11 attacks; since then, this woman—a Jewish grandmother in her sixties—had been interrogated and searched every time she flew.

I thought, What if calls to Iran . . .? and such questions deterred me from pursuing my investigation further, for the time being.

Christmas arrived, and I entered a particularly difficult period of grief.

I dreamed I was staying in a castle. I went to a stone balcony, seeking solitude to cry over my mom. Down in the Hudson River I saw a triangular barge full of bloodhounds, from which a man emerged riding an ATV, which he drove up the riverbank. Was a puppy in his briefcase?

I mention this to demonstrate the utterly baffling nature of my bereavement, a process that seemed to be happening somewhere beyond my purview—if indeed it was a process, moving toward any sort of change or resolution.

As if arriving at the hospital "in time" would have made any difference.

Mainly that winter I was consumed or overwhelmed by the details of daily life, such as my duties at the magazine, which happened to be particularly odious just then.

You could say my own sense of loss felt foreign to me.

Nothing much John could do, besides hug me.

"Oh, Kid," he'd say, rubbing my back.

I wrote things in my journal like, "Silence of grief, effort of such, silent effort, indescribable—'hole,' etc."

I passed in and out of this state all winter.

*

According to www.setar.info, "Setar, in Persian, means 'three strings,' but a fourth one was added by Moshtaq Ali Shah, a famous setar player of the 18th century. This 'sympathetic' string is not played but its echo highlights the predominant note . . ."

In me, the mystery items from Iran had found a sympathetic string.

One day in March I realized I could probably locate a Farsi speaker easily on Craigslist; in ten seconds I had found two.

Next I looked on my phone card's website and saw a very reasonable rate for Iran: clearly people called there all the time.

This sudden can-do spirit was possibly a sign of improving mental health.

I e-mailed the Farsi speaker with a recent degree in translation from the University of Tehran.

Farahnaz—Fari for short—called me the next day. I hadn't realized until then that she was female. She had only a slight accent and seemed suitably amused by the idea of telephoning a shoe store in Tehran for me.

Indeed my story sounded so much like an e-mail scam (I just need the number of your bank account, and then I can return the lute music to its rightful owner . . .) that I was grateful to Fari for replying at all.

It appeared to say something about her character.

I asked her about her own experience coming to the United States, and she told of watching with trepidation as a guard in Turkey emptied her backpack onto a table: "All my valuables were in the bag—my documents, jewelry, everything. I thought, 'My stuff! Be careful!' Of course I thought they were only doing it because I'm Iranian. I take everything so personally."

This charmed me.

*

Once again I relied on the auspices of the magazine to make my investigation appear legit: I arranged for Fari to meet me at my office that Friday morning.

As I waited for her, a siren echoed up from 57th Street.

Though I had prepared myself for a stern-looking girl in a headscarf, Fari arrived wearing a light green sweater and brown corduroys. She had shoulder-length hair and that pretty curlicue nose you see in Persian and Indian paintings.

She had brought along her American husband, Brian, a short, studious-looking guy in a slack gray suit and round wire-frame glasses. He explained he was on his way to the placement office at NYU, where he had been a graduate student in sociology.

I asked them to tell me about themselves. They had met the previous year on German Friendster, when Brian was in Germany doing research and Fari was there visiting relatives. They were married a few months later, in Turkey, and had just moved to Yonkers.

"OK, I guess we should get started," I said, and I poured the contents of the shopping bag onto the white Formica.

Fari's smile was somehow both sly and demure, and she seemed perpetually amused. Maybe this is common among exiles.

When Brian picked up the red woman's dress and asked, "Is this the sort of thing a woman in Iran would wear shopping?", Fari smiled with pursed lips, as if this were the dumbest question in the world. "I'm just asking," Brian said, but he didn't seem to mind the teasing.

He's in love, I thought.

"She would be wearing that to some kind of gathering," Fari resumed. "She's trying to look nice wearing that. It's like the nicest thing she could come up with." I admired this bit of fashion criticism, which confirmed that Fari would be helpful beyond mere translation.

But Brian was the one who thought to look closely at the labels on the dress, noting the "Made in U.S.A." A good clue that our mystery family lived somewhere in the United States, or at least had relatives here.

I hadn't noticed the dress size either: 14 Petite.

Fari tapped the fake jewel on the scimitar pin. "This says a lot," she said. "What kind of woman would wear a sword?" Chuckling, I asked what she meant. "The sword," she replied, "is a religious thing—it belongs to one of the prophets." Which prophet? "Ali, I think."

I gathered from this that Fari herself wasn't particularly religious, and I assumed this had been a problem for her in Iran.

Turning to the music books, she noted the same copyright date on all three, 1385 on the Persian calendar, or the current year, which was about to end (at the vernal equinox).

We reasoned, therefore, that the music was probably purchased in Iran, just prior to the flight on which it was lost. The books were instructional, Fari added, so evidently someone the woman knew must have wanted to learn the setar—maybe one of the children?

I tried to extrapolate from my own childhood—lute lessons, instead of flute.

Their colorful costumes included both skirts and pants, so I had concluded one kid was a boy, but Fari informed me that they had to be two girls: the skirts would be worn over the pants. The three of us agreed the children were probably nine or ten.

Fari believed a tailor had made the outfits, which would have been inexpensive in Iran. Brian wondered if the tailor might have been near the shoe store, and Fari thought this plausible.

What were the costumes for? I asked. "Something religious, maybe a religious play," Fari replied. I tried to picture this but drew a blank.

"Green would be a religious color," she continued, holding up the pants that were emerald with gold trim. "The Prophet is often described wearing that color." I asked whether the children would sing or recite or what. Again she wasn't sure, by which I inferred she had never attended such a gathering.

"The store's name means 'Genius,'" she announced. She was looking closely now at the shopping bag. Was it an upscale shop? "I've never been to it, but no. It's not on a street where rich people go to buy stuff. And maybe it's not even bad to buy cheaper stuff," she added—a possible reference to compromises such as Yonkers.

At the bottom of the bag was a newspaper from Tehran, which Fari described as "kind of left wing but not very much. This one has been able to survive, because it isn't too left wing. I did some translations for newspapers that were shut down because they were too left wing."

Later she told me she had wanted to be a TV journalist, but this had been virtually impossible for her, "because of my family." Unclear what she meant—too liberal, not religious enough, or what.

Brian left for his appointment at NYU, and I showed Fari my list of questions for the shoe store. Though I had worried it would be closed on a Friday evening, she assured me everything would be open in the weeks leading up to the Persian New Year.

It took several tries to connect. At last she began speaking Farsi and chuckling as she explained the reason for her call. I could tell she had struck just the right tone to enlist their help. She gestured with her pen as she talked and jotted a note now and then. She wrote with her left hand, right to left. Soon she put her palm over the mouthpiece. "He says,

'I don't know any tailor around here. I don't know how to help you.' But he's talking to his dad and his brother," she explained. "Their name is Ferdoos" (pronounced fair-dose). In a moment she relayed to me the man's suggestion that I mail the bag to the store so that he could show the lost items to his customers. I countered that it would be better if I e-mailed him photos of the items. "OK, he's looking for someone who has an e-mail address," Fari said. In a moment she began speaking into the phone again, murmuring what sounded like "Bai . . . Bai" and chuckling some more. She copied down an e-mail address, said a cordial-sounding something, and hung up.

"They were very nice people!" she exclaimed, beaming. "I enjoyed speaking Farsi!"

Until then I hadn't realized that, in many ways, she must miss Iran.

The second conversation, Fari explained, was with the brother. "He told me to send the pictures," she said, "and he'll print them and ask their customers." I had already photographed the items, so I proposed doing the e-mail now. She said she would write it in "Pinglish," or Farsi in Western script.

"It's interesting," she continued, turning from my phone to my keyboard. "I was not really hoping to get anywhere. I was thinking maybe if there had been shoes in the bag . . . But I knew the shop would be open, because this is a time that they sell a lot of clothes."

I asked if people gave presents for New Year's, like Christmas here. "Mmm, it's not like here," she replied. "Everybody buys clothes for themselves, and parents buy clothes for their kids, but not as a present. At the New Year they want to have nice clothes on. This year it's at 3 a.m. They have to get up very early in the morning." She laughed, wistfully, I thought.

"It's exciting to get up in the middle of the night to celebrate," she said. Was it a party, like New Year's Eve in the West? "No, it's more like a family thing. At the New Year you want to be with your family."

She explained various other aspects of the holiday, such as its being not a Muslim custom, but a Zoroastrian one.

She mentioned jumping over a fire, to which you give illness and take health.

She described a table on which are placed seven items that all begin with the Persian letter *s*, including a coin, an apple, a particular kind of fish, a certain flower. "They each have meaning, I'm not sure what, but they have good meaning," she said.

The advantage of staying in your home country, I thought, was that you didn't need to know your own traditions too thoroughly. If Fari wanted to recreate her traditions here, with Brian, she would have to ask her mother about them, in detail.

I wasn't thinking about my own lost traditions just then, or about my own mother; I didn't have to, because I was thinking about Fari.

*

We tried sending the e-mail but it wouldn't go through. Fari agreed to send a letter for me instead, enclosing printouts of the photographs. I doubted we would hear back (and we never did).

Meanwhile, my sympathy for the shopping bag's rightful owners, already transposed from my grief over my mother, had, in turn, been transposed to Fari.

In a way. But it had all been in a way, anyway.

Whatever the reason, I had connected with this young woman and her story, and whether or not this was momentary or the beginning of a friendship, I felt obscurely satisfied.

As if you could find success entirely by analogy.

The various consolations life hands you, from unexpected quarters.

My mother's pastor had said it was as if my mother wanted to spare me the pain of actually seeing her die.

"It's okay to touch her," the pastor added, and for the last time I took my mother's hand.

As Fari prepared to go meet Brian, I impulsively gave her a copy of my novel about Winkie.

In it, I thank my mother for giving me her childhood teddy bear.

Fari said she didn't know the bus system in New York City

and was afraid of getting lost, so I walked her down to the stop and carefully explained which route to take.

As we looked up Eighth Avenue I felt motherly, wanting Fari to succeed in America.

Rain had begun to fall, so I also gave her my umbrella.

KEN

1

MY BROTHER'S MERCURY Zephyr handled so poorly that whenever he rounded a tight corner he used to say, "Here comes the Queen Mary."

Once he and his good friend Jeff were having lunch outdoors and a sparrow began aggressively fluttering around Ken's head, so from then on Jeff started calling him Tippi.

Jeff recalls that the two of them also laughed that day in San Diego about the image of Tippi Hedren out in a rowboat on Bodega Bay, in heels and a full-length mink.

Ken died of AIDS in 1989. A few years later I published a book about it, titled *The Hurry-Up Song*.

I say "about *it*" instead of about "about *him*" because the book is a portrait of the author losing his brother, rather than a portrait of the brother himself. Whatever the reader sees of Ken is exclusively from my point of view.

Almost as if reflected in my glasses.

I didn't interview any of his friends for the book, and

though I knew my mother had kept his journal, I didn't ask to read it.

I felt I couldn't take into account the grief of his friends in addition to my own, nor could I absorb any more of his suffering than I had already witnessed.

Thus not only was the published portrait of Ken lacking, but my own idea of him remained incomplete, and perhaps by extension, so was my grief.

I was also afraid of finding out he was angry with me when he died, which wasn't a wild guess, since he was very angry toward the end.

In my Waspy way I thought it was better not to know.

The avoidance accounts for much of the twelve-year gap in this narrative, between E. and John.

But now, more than twenty years after Ken's death, I find myself willing to read his diary and to ask for the recollections of his friends.

That willingness is somehow related to having cared for my parents, and lost them. Hence for me Ken's diary takes place now as much as in the 1980s.

His journal entries are fragmentary, as are memories, but I hope this portrait will be fuller than the earlier attempt.

2

"DREAM," HE WRITES, in February 1984: "Surrealistic acid-like feeling of stumbling through my bedroom, trying to get somewhere and not being able to." He offers no interpretation.

He hadn't yet tested positive, but my first thought is that the dream foreshadows his futile struggle with HIV.

In fact, it simply expresses frustration with his love life at that moment.

When I refer to Ken's journal, I actually mean a series of small black vinyl notebooks running from early 1984 to mid-1987, continuing with a sheaf of larger, unlined pages in which dates quickly disappear altogether.

His handwriting: a slightly more extravagant version of my own.

He records nothing in the way of physical setting, music he liked, or current events, though regarding the news, I recall that he read the paper every day.

As for weather, there was little for him to report, since the climate in San Diego is so mild. Palms and yuccas punctuate the streets. Year-round, the air smells of flowers.

My perusal of the *San Diego Union* during the eighties reveals a parade of homophobia, not only in the news itself (an anti-gay protestor carrying a sign that reads "Got AIDS

Yet?"), but in how gays and lesbians are covered (phrases like "admitted homosexual" and "the militant homosexual community").

Ken's likely reaction: sarcasm. "Chahhh-ming," he used to say, like Katharine Hepburn opening a lovely gift.

His sense of humor is another thing excluded from his notebooks.

In 1984 he had recently begun psychotherapy (both individual and group), which I assume was his reason for starting the diary.

He met Jeff in the group, whose members were all gay men. Jeff says they were encouraged to see each other outside of therapy and even to have sex if they liked. (I don't ask if he and Ken did.)

Ken was a mathematician and computer analyst, and much of the journal is comprised of numbered lists of feelings, such as this entry from that April:

> 1) Extreme agitation over psychotherapy bills. Feeling cry-ish all day. Lack of appetite. Anger, sadness, sulky, butterflies in stomach
> 2) Anger at group—lack of support from all but Phil [the group therapist]. Negative reactions to comment that I was bored (e.g. 'You distance yourself from the group" . . .)
> Highly negative criticisms of my mannerisms

I want to reach back and protect him from the other members of his group, from his tears and his butterflies.

He was always worried about money (especially after he got sick), so that same month he decided to quit individual therapy and continue only with group, presumably because it was cheaper and despite continued complaints in his journal such as "They won't *listen* to me."

My own therapist during the eighties wouldn't allow me to call him by his first name, and we had virtually no rapport—which, as I recall, felt weirdly safe.

My own trying to get somewhere and not being able to. My own feeling that no one would listen to me.

This line, also from April 1984, could have been written by me: "When I have 'gut' (affective) stuff going on inside I don't have good access to it (or none at all!), so I have trouble expressing myself."

A "Dear Abby" column Ken taped to the page: "DEAR CON-FUSED: You have been using sex to fill an unmet emotional need that's been gnawing at you since you were very young."

Like me Ken had a lot of bad childhood memories. One Wednesday when he was little, our older brother Paul and his friend Billy told Ken that it was Saturday, not Wednesday, and as he tried to object, they sang "Saturday! Saturday! Saturday!" over and over until he started to scream.

In turn Ken sometimes tortured me—the "invisible" episode and countless socks on the arm—but he and I also had a lot in common and often played together—I owe my sense of humor to him—so my memories of him are profoundly mixed.

On the same page as "Dear Abby," Ken considers asking out a guy named Art.

"Need for an emotionally fulfilling relationship," he writes on April 21. "Anger and hurt regarding past sexual experiences . . . The emotional fulfillment was lacking and I felt very cheated since I was looking for something that was not part of the implicit social contract."

I remember Ken once bragging that he took home only the "prettiest" guys at the bar, but evidently he wanted something different now.

In 1984 I was still vacillating over E.

Front-page news, April 24: discovery of the AIDS virus, development of a blood test, prediction of a vaccine within two years. I wonder if this false optimism affected Ken positively.

In early May he reports that he "fucked with Arthur for first time. First he did me then I did him."

The threshold for writing down good things appears to be very high—the diary is concerned almost entirely with problems—so I conclude that fucking with Arthur must have been not simply a good experience but an extraordinary one.

Or was it, in fact, a problem? That same night he dreams: "Intruder in the house, I overpower him and throw him out; return to bedroom to find Art gone; realize ejected one was Art; return to front door, call him back and he returns to me . . ."

Wanting love, and fearing love.

Later that month Ken dreams that "Arthur left a message on answering machine saying that he loved me and wanted to live with me."

Regarding an unspecified quarrel: "Called Arthur and told him of my 'distress' after our talk Sunday. Also told him I romanticize and like being in love . . . Phrase he used: 'stages going through while developing a closer relationship.'"

The hopefulness of this. Arthur's apparent sensibleness. The possibility that their romance might endure.

3

IN MY PHONE conversation with him, Arthur recalls: "There were definitely some difficult things that happened while we were dating, as though we were kind of working out the connection. It was a little rough. That wasn't the part that was important to me, that there were problems."

Arthur's reply to the letter I had sent said he was glad to hear from me because he still had "unresolved feelings" toward Ken.

He had owned a copy of *The Hurry-Up Song* for a number of years but coincidentally had only read it a couple of months earlier.

"Twenty Years After Ken's Death" appeared to be a mathematical function at work in others besides myself.

"I have these pictures of him in my mind," Arthur tells me. "I can see him in certain places."

I wonder if Ken somehow spawned unresolved feelings more than most people do.

I ask Arthur how they met. "Well, you know, this is another one of those moments I can remember absolutely. We were going to a gym in Mission Valley. I think it was the Holiday Spa at the time. I was standing at the desk looking over my exercise card to get started that day, and here comes Ken. This cute blond guy comes up, and it was like, hi." He laughs. "We started chatting, and he wanted to get together and he wanted to exchange phone numbers. That was the beginning."

Both Jeff and another friend of Ken's, Jim, similarly refer to Ken as a "hunk."

Arthur himself had thick dark hair and a dark mustache. He was about Ken's height, five-seven.

"I don't remember our first date," says Arthur. "We did end up back over at his apartment [in Ocean Beach, where Arthur also lived]. There was the surfboard. It was just—it was kind of basic. I didn't know too much about him at that point. We spent the night together . . . I was looking for at least a solid dating relationship, to see where it would go. We did an awful lot together. I'm remembering some parties we went to. Various things."

Are there other pictures in his mind? "Oh," he laughs. "One night he came over to my apartment. I was standing in the kitchen and my roommate Ray was there. Ken comes in and he's got this bouquet of flowers. I was nonplussed—some guy is bringing me flowers. It kind of startled me. He said, 'Oh,

I guess this is a little too much for you.' No one had ever done that for me."

"Ken and I would be out, we'd stop for coffee, encountering friends [of mine], and they'd say, 'Wow, your boyfriend is really cute.' I hadn't thought of him as some trophy husband. He was a nice guy, down to earth, very bright. His vocabulary was, you know, impressive. We could talk intelligently about things."

Jim also remarked on how easy it was to talk to my brother. Since Jim was on the board of a major AIDS organization, they used to discuss the rancorous gay politics in San Diego.

"There were these expressions he had that were distinctly his," says Arthur. I don't need to ask for examples because I know Ken's distinct expressions so well—such as "Nards!" when he was mildly annoyed; or "Oh, Mitch" for a slow driver who got in his way (after an incompetent super he once had); or "Cheap-cheap-cheap," high-pitched like a bird, when he didn't want to spend money.

"Ken definitely had a different perspective," Arthur continues. "It was one of the things I really liked about him."

In June of that year Ken moved into the house in San Diego where he would die—a one-bedroom Spanish bungalow, built in the twenties, with a crenulated façade. The matching one-car garage resembled a little stucco castle.

"He wanted us to live together," Arthur says. "And I was, like, right on the edge of that. And it was just like, please, don't push too much right now. Just give me some—I felt like I needed a little more time to get accustomed to the idea.

Because he was the last of three really significant guys that I dated." I assume Arthur means he was still getting over the previous two relationships. Immediately he goes on to say, "After him, I only dated somebody again in the mid-nineties, almost ten years later."

4

AN INDEX CARD in the envelope containing Ken's diary notes, "June '84—1st tested positive," but there's no mention of this event in the diary itself.

The general atmosphere back then of panic, stigma, fury, and denial regarding HIV, which wasn't even yet called HIV.

Rev. Jerry Falwell famously called it the "gay plague."

Possibly Ken feared someone finding his journal and learning of his HIV status. He worked in the defense industry and had a security clearance, so he remained closeted at work.

Each weekday evening, the pink neon sign for his neighborhood—Normal Heights—appeared in his windshield, signaling his arrival in a less secretive zone.

He did talk about his test result with Arthur, soon after he learned of it. "Oh, oh, oh, here's the critical event," Arthur recalls. "We were in the water bed one evening and he said, 'You know I was at the doctor's and I found out that I'm positive.' And we'd been not exclusively top or bottom—I guess it would be like people who really do get into a relationship—it was very mutual, not role playing. And we weren't using any condoms." So Arthur figured he must have been positive too (which indeed he is, though I don't ask when he found out for sure). "The thing was, the two guys I'd dated prior to this also became positive, and I can't remember if I knew that before I was dating Ken. I don't think so."

Ken had received his HIV test as part of a scientific study. In addition to the index card, there's a letter from UCSD Medical Center, which cautions, ". . . we are not yet sure of the significance of these test results."

I don't know how many other people Ken told. There's no hint in the journal that he talked about it in group therapy. He didn't tell me until sometime in 1986, and my parents did not find out until he actually landed in the hospital, in the fall of 1987.

In the entry dated June 18/19, 1984, Ken writes:

> depression
> ambivalence
> feelings of being overwhelmed by house
> feeling trapped
> . . .
> Focusing on memory of helping Dad paint living room in house in Conn. And getting in trouble for getting paint on floor while trying to paint the quarter round.

My parents' tirades over such minor infractions were so common that Ken and I drew cartoons about them.

By "June 18/19" he must mean it's about midnight, and he can't sleep. I imagine him writing at the pale, rectangular dining table from the forties that had belonged to my parents. The windows were probably open to the balmy air, since according to the almanac, the low that night was sixty-six.

It was cloudy every morning that week—a San Diego weather pattern known as "June Gloom."

June 22: "Issue for next private session: difficulty in cumming while having sex with other guys. Difficulty fucking. Ambivalence re getting fucked."

The following month he records a timetable of the men he's been with—perhaps trying to determine when he seroconverted, perhaps simply taking stock of his love life.

At San Diego's Gay Pride parade earlier that month, a plane had towed an anti-gay banner above Balboa Park. In mid-July, demonstrators near the Democratic National Convention in San Francisco demanded more federal funding for AIDS research. I assume Ken couldn't participate in such events, since that would have risked his security clearance. On the other hand, I don't recall his ever saying he'd like to attend gay parades or protests.

July 20: ". . . very depressed; cried for no reason; unable to concentrate; disinterest in work/Art/house; lack of appetite . . ."

I don't know how much of this he shared with Arthur. Ken's friend Jim tells me he never talked about his darker feelings, but Jim could sense they were there.

July 20, continued: "Becoming more and more angry at anything and everything . . . culminating in Thursday—felt 'compulsion' to get stoned. However, decided consciously not to."

This is the first time the journal brings up pot. Eventually Ken would come to see it as a serious addiction, and he would become very active in both Narcotics Anonymous and AA.

Arthur tells me that he himself had been sober for several years when he met Ken. I'm surprised because Ken never mentions this fact in his journal.

Arthur doesn't recall ever seeing him get high, nor even smelling it on him: "I don't know when he was doing it." Evidently Ken was making an effort to hide it. Sometime later, after they had broken up, Arthur was quite surprised to see him at an AA meeting. (This is one of the vivid pictures in Arthur's mind.) If my brother's addiction was as powerful and pernicious as he eventually concluded, then not smoking in front of Arthur—presumably because Arthur was in AA—must have made spending time with him difficult. Yet the journal never mentions this as a factor in their relations.

July 23: "Still some sores in mouth"—first mention of possible HIV-related symptoms, though Ken remained healthy for another year and a half.

August 6: "Saw Arthur today. He told me I had forced emotional growth in him, which was hard for him. We will continue seeing each other, see what happens."

But on August 10 Ken writes: "Arthur called. . . . I felt like I was forcing my affections on him."

Regardless of Arthur's probable HIV status, the virus may have made Ken feel tainted. This would have been hard to admit, let alone discuss.

August 12: "Dragged someone home from the bar; finally decided I was comfortable with him here; slept cuddled up; very nice."

Not that I want to deny Ken this nice evening, but it does appear to have been a distraction from Arthur.

Presumably Ken didn't reveal his HIV status to this anonymous someone.

"Saturday . . . told Art I didn't want to go to dinner . . . woke up feeling alone and lonely and missing Art."

Later in August, he writes of "seeing Art stringing me along indefinitely in his ambivalence and then suddenly dumping me. Fear of abandonment?"

Ken had had tantrums as a kid, and my mother sometimes left him alone for long periods—as he shrieked and cried. My sister Helen has a similar story. I did not have tantrums, but my childhood was marked in its own way by my mother's particular brand of moody, sporadic attention.

August 15: ". . . feel like getting stoned and escaping everything . . . realizing that I wanted to get stoned to escape *feeling*. Recall the implicit message of childhood—'don't feel.'"

5

PONDERING THAT STATEMENT makes me emotional.

Anger on his behalf. Also a sense of confirmation—as I often felt when Ken and I talked about the family. Hence renewed sadness that we can no longer have such conversations.

To be clear, "don't feel" wasn't always the message. Sometimes we got sympathy, sometimes derision, sometimes indifference, depending on the feelings we expressed, depending on our parents' moods.

What Ken confirms is the uncertainty, the constant self-doubt.

My mother liked to tell a story of how my sister Helen once fell down and skinned her knee but did not start crying until she saw my mother. To her, this meant Helen didn't actually feel significant pain but was merely "trying to get attention."

Wanting attention was the feeling my mother considered most suspect.

With similar myopia, I had difficulty accepting Ken's decision to pursue abstinence. I considered pot the least of his troubles and wrote derisively of Narcotics Anonymous in *The Hurry-Up Song*, calling the program an extreme solution to a minor problem.

But now, as I read the words "don't feel," suddenly I understand. Pot was sopping up his unwanted emotions, and he decided he didn't want to live that way anymore.

The journal itself is a forum for those unwanted emotions.

As if to reward himself for this new insight, that same day, August 15, 1984, Ken goes on to recount a moment of ordinary happiness: "Jeff Wynne called at 8 p.m.—joked with him and felt better."

In five years of journal entries, this is one of only three mentions of Jeff, which I assume indicates, paradoxically, just how important Jeff's friendship was to him as a source of unfreighted everyday cheerfulness.

August 19:

> . . . irrational fear Arthur was going to stand me up.
>
> . . . but enjoyed movie; also sex was very good, and worked without working at it. Sunday morning felt in very strange mood, talked about [it] to Arthur and felt better.
>
> . . . Also went to [a restaurant] for a snack . . . Art revealed that he felt uncomfortable there, like someone was making comments about us. Then he got mad at me and that made me feel hurt, but I didn't tell him that (why not?) . . .

Cf. my secrets in Egypt.

Still, on August 21 Ken acknowledges that Arthur has "opened up" to him (though he doesn't note how) and that such disclosures are "the building blocks of intimacy and a serious relationship."

August 23:

> Thinking about last night's dinner with Arthur—
> . . .
> Our brief talk about our feelings about the events of the day
> The feeling of peace and contentment after dinner

Six days later he writes: "Payoff of my anger is withdrawal. Withdrawal is 'safe'; because it puts me into an 'invincible' and 'invulnerable' position."

Again, the psychic flavor is very close to my own, like red raspberries vs. yellow. (For example: a late childhood memory of hiding in my bedroom closet after an argument with Ken himself.)

That month Ken also writes of "a fear that if people see the real me they won't like what they see and/or they will then know what openings to use in order to 'get' to me."

My own persistent belief that whenever I feel good, someone is bound to come along and deflate me.

On August 31 Ken writes: "Making love to Arthur was *wonderful* Thursday. I was holding his cock and he was holding mine, but it was feeling so good, it was as if I was not sure if I was holding him or myself."

Then once again a nightmare: "Outside, a backyard with a solid fence & a gate. Satan is behind gate. [I'm] pounding on the gate, tempting Satan to come get me. He starts to come for me, I barely escape. I wake up scared."

The deeply destabilizing influence of HIV; the deeply destabilizing influence of childhood.

I picture the high redwood slats surrounding Ken's concrete backyard, or the fence around the yard in San Jose.

In early September the *San Diego Union* reported that a member of the county board of supervisors had expressed concern that improved services "for homosexuals with AIDS might attract other victims of the deadly disorder to the region."

However Ken reacted to such stories, as I read through them I feel like I'm watching him get kicked.

September 20: ". . . Not feeling good about myself . . . Wondering why I am not enough for Arthur . . ."

October 10: ". . . fear of a world full of ogres . . ."

Later in October he recounts various small tiffs with Arthur. To me, the disagreements don't appear insurmountable—but I say this with many more years of life experience than Ken had as of 1984. He was thirty-two. I'm now fifty-two. I've been with John seventeen years, with all their ups and downs.

And then there's the fact that I'm not facing a life-threatening disease.

Later that fall, Ken mentions wanting to talk to his therapist about someone named Bill, so he must have been seeing him on the side.

Knowing what I now know about Arthur, I can't help but view this, again, as an evasion. Ken dated both Bill and Arthur for the next several months, seeming to grow more and more convinced that he preferred Bill.

Jeff describes Bill as "very cute" but "not the brightest bulb."

January 8, 1985:

    1) Bill loves me

2) I must reach completion with Arthur

3) Bill hates to be the other woman

4) Bill hates it when Ken holds back

5) Bill wants to suck Ken's cock with a rubber on because he's scared to death of the unknown.

"Bill loves me"—and by implication Arthur doesn't? But unless Arthur is now wildly romanticizing the past, Ken couldn't have been more wrong.

Possibly at some point he told me about these two men, and if so, he would have couched things in just this way, so that I would have advised him to go with Bill.

January 19: "Why is Arthur never happy when he's with me? Why do I make him crazy?"

Arthur tells me that when he met Ken, he had only recently moved into his own apartment, after years of living with roommates. He had also recently gone back to college and then dropped out again. "So I felt like I was still getting my bearings," he recalls. "I felt like his house would be good for a couple, and even so it felt a bit small. He even said, 'We can find a bigger house to rent and I can rent my house out.' He was thinking how to work this out. I was like, OK, good—and suddenly it was 'I can't do this anymore, I have to stop dating you.'"

No mention of this conversation in Ken's journal. Was he trying not to think about it?

"I can't say it was devastating, that sounds so dramatic," Arthur continues. "It was just so unsettling. I said, 'Can't we just continue on a bit? I'm close but I'm not quite there yet.' He went back to seeing someone I knew very casually [Bill], who I think he'd been dating before. I couldn't understand it other than he felt he needed to break the connection with me because I wasn't ready to move as quickly as he was. He had just bought this house. It was a really cute little house."

Possibly I hear Arthur sniffle. I'm afraid if I speak my voice will crack.

He was so surprised by Ken's decision that he briefly resorted to stalking him: "Because I was so upset about this and couldn't believe this was happening . . . I can laugh about [the stalking] now because it's like a movie of the week. One day I drove over to 35th Street [where Ken lived]. I saw Ken's car, so I was like following him. There was someone else in the car, and I could tell it was Bill. Then I realized they knew I was following them. They turned [a corner], and I thought, 'I've got to stop doing this.'"

Even in this story of questionable behavior, I see Arthur's self-awareness in stark contrast to the picture of Bill that soon emerges in Ken's journal—and from the bitter things Ken said to me about Bill later.

Late in February, "a sticky white rain fell across Southern California," reports the National Weather Service, which attributes the unusual phenomenon to desert dust blown by high winds into rainclouds. Characteristically, Ken's diary makes no reference to this event. I picture him hosing the storm's white, gritty residue from his driveway.

As it turned out, Bill was Ken's final boyfriend.

Arthur: "That night that he said, 'I'm positive, I knew I had to tell you this'—it was kind of one of those moments you get very thoughtful and real about life. And when I was reading your book, it really hit, because I thought—I got the feeling that here's this person who wanted me to live with him and I couldn't quite do it fast enough. And when I was reading about his [negative] attitude about taking medicine, I wished I could have been there. . . But it's always what might have happened."

6

ON MARCH 11, 1985, a dream: "Judge is talking to me about trust. He says to trust and extends his hand, when I reach for it he pulls it back, he then talks about trust again, extends his hand and says trust me, take my hand; I refuse to reach for his hand."

The entry continues:

> Very difficult to read Bill and what he wanted/wants. Sometimes he says he wishes I were more forceful but when I am he refuses to submit . . .
>
> Bill is selfish, inconsiderate, thoughtless, rude. His insecurity manifests itself as insensitivity . . .
>
> 1) "Don't take my Valium!"
>   "I'm only taking one."
> 2) Turning off TV without asking (twice), turned off light.
> 3) Sunday night I wanted reciprocal cuddling and he wouldn't do it.
> 4) He will not stop teasing me, will not stop saying I look "reptilian."
> 5) He is CHEAP.

Ken records these scenes with a specificity rare in his journal. Maybe he hopes to convince himself that Bill really is that awful. Indeed, entries of this sort continue for several more months.

My theory is that Bill enjoyed stealing Ken away from Arthur but, once he got him, didn't want him anymore.

Again I feel protective of Ken, angry with him, embarrassed for him. Embarrassed because of the resemblance to my own love life back then, starting with the creep I was seeing that same year (my boyfriend before G.)—the impossibility of getting more than the tiniest amounts of affection from him, and how that impossibility mesmerized me for months. (After we broke up I had my own dream about a judge, in this case explicitly my father, before whom I made an impassioned argument that the dog didn't have to be left home all day alone.)

On April 10 Ken writes, "Tonight he hung up on me."

April 25: ". . . the lack of sympathy when I tell him about something that's bothering me. He either gets mad at me, criticizes me or makes fun of me . . ."

In May, a list of Bill's good and bad traits.

In late June a fire erupted in a canyon next to Normal Heights and destroyed seventy-six homes. Ken doesn't mention this, though I recall he had to evacuate. Did he take refuge with Bill?

In August AIDS appeared on the covers of both *Time* and the magazine I worked for. "No one has ever recovered from the disease," reads the latter, under a photo of actor Rock Hudson's ravaged face. I, for one, was now officially terrified.

In September, Bill's "consistent refusal to hold me when I want to be held."

Later in September: "The feeling that I will never experience the closeness that I want."

It's precisely this despair that tempts me to hold back with John: a damning certainty that he can't give me what I want.

The day after Christmas: "Bill is completely incapable of dealing with feelings . . . However, *he doesn't think it's a problem.*"

G. was similarly uncomfortable with emotion. Not that he lacked good qualities, but for four years I was always trying to figure him out, doubting myself, hoping to stretch his brief moments of tenderness into something more.

In late December Ken decided once and for all to stop smoking pot. In January he asks, "Why am I so drawn to this relationship where I constantly have excuses to be angry all the time? Answer: alcoholic behavior! When I collect enough anger points, then I get stoned. And when I am so angry, and then I smoke pot, it gets me really high. When I smoke it when I am not angry like this, I can't get stoned enough."

My own penchant for squirreling away indignation, reserving it for imaginary arguments. Similarly, Ken refers (elsewhere in his journal) to "vignettes" in which "I am the 'triumphant' orator brutally crushing the 'fool' who didn't do what I wanted him to do, regardless of the fact that my desires were not well articulated. I then stomp out the door in disgust . . ."

In an undated entry from the spring of 1986, he writes, "What do I really want from life, the universe and everything?" It's around this time that he finally breaks up with Bill.

He also starts recording various symptoms—a sore throat, a rash, "continuous mental fog all afternoon," "sore gums," "fatigue: mild."

Another undated entry:

> How you feel about death:
> . . . locked in a white room with no windows and no door.

But on June 23 he writes: "Getting some insight over the anger I still feel toward Bill. It's OK to feel that anger . . . to experience its exact texture; but it's not good to be paralyzed by it."

He has traveled all the way from "don't feel" to "experience its exact texture."

7

AS KEN GREW sicker, his personality became increasingly distorted by terror, rage, and self-hatred.

His illness also warped my memories of him, overshadowing all that came before.

The diary becomes increasingly difficult to read, and I have to tell myself over and over that it isn't the whole story.

The collective white space here represents several months in 2009 and 2010 of trying to absorb and understand his suffering.

July 30, 1986:

> Just feeling so crummy about myself . . .
> Getting very depressed over my health problems.
> Getting very depressed over the red splotchy spots on
> my face.

Front page news: the Supreme Court upheld Georgia's anti-sodomy law, five to four.

Local news: after a gay man bit two San Diego policemen during an altercation, prosecutors sought to test his blood for HIV without his consent, in case the charge could be upgraded from simple battery to attempted murder.

August 12: "My self-esteem is fragile—[Bill's] constant criticism . . . left me feeling just like I did as a child when Paul would pick at me."

Every night Ken went to a meeting of either NA or AA.

He grew increasingly unhappy at work.

November 14: ". . . my need to never make a mistake and thus avoid criticism . . ."

December 15: "Situation: car in shop for repairs . . . Why does it upset me so much?"

I found his irritability over such things hard to take. It felt like we were never talking about the real problem, his health.

His irritability also resembled my mother's from when I was a kid.

I imagine my own reaction to a terminal illness would be similar.

February 14, 1987: "1) My fear of people. When someone looks at me, a stab of fear goes through my heart/stomach. Why? How to overcome? . . ."

On April 1 Ronald Reagan advised abstinence and monogamy to combat AIDS, adding, ". . . don't medicine and morality teach the same lessons?"

That spring Ken lost his job, for which he blamed himself.

Months passed. He accepted a position up in San Jose and found a buyer for his house in San Diego.

Then, after much agonizing—I had several phone conversations with him about it—he changed his mind and took a job in San Diego instead.

On some level he must have realized he wasn't physically able to make such a big change. But he had to pay a penalty to the buyer of his house, and the episode left him feeling humiliated and defeated.

My mother had very much wanted him to move to San Jose.

He considered going on an antidepressant but decided against it, possibly influenced by the sternest faction of Narcotics Anonymous.

He decided to try AZT, which had been approved by the FDA earlier that year.

October 29: "I am well and healthy," written eleven times.

That weekend my parents celebrated their 50th wedding anniversary, in San Jose, but Ken was unable to come because he had the flu.

Undated entry: A drawing of a drip with stick legs, its stick arms manipulating some dark spots in a circle. Then the same figure again, smiling, with thought balloon, "Zippity dooda zippity-ay . . ."

Undated: "I am frustrated and angry about being sick for so long. Powerless."

November 10: ". . . 3) I am healthy and well," written seven times.

November 13: "I am so fucking lazy and so fucking cheap."

November 15:

> 99.4 [evidently his temperature]
> . . .
> I feel very frustrated over this current episode and very frightened. [wild handwriting]
> . . . I am bored. By getting sick I create excitement and attention.

Evidently he had been reading Louise Hay, whose books prescribe "positive ideas" to fight any disease.

Three days later he went into the hospital with what turned out to be pneumocystis. Thus he was formally diagnosed with "full-blown" AIDS.

He received this news in a brusque phone call from his internist.

On Jeff's advice, he telephoned my parents, and they headed down to San Diego to take care of him when he got home. This was heroic of them, though they didn't tell me or my siblings that Ken had been hospitalized. I didn't find out until I tried calling him, wondering why I hadn't heard from him lately, and my mother answered his phone. "Mom?" I said.

November 24: He plans to talk to his sponsor about having taken a single sleeping pill.

November 28: "5) Must completely turn life around; fill it with love and health and wonderful people . . ."

In a letter to me, he writes of stirring conversations with my parents about being gay and his addiction to pot. At the time, his confessional mood struck me as abject, and I wished he hadn't shared with Mom and Dad the part about NA.

I myself wasn't yet out to my parents.

Given their right-wing views, I had never expected a good reaction. Now I wondered if they had accepted Ken only because he was sick.

We had Christmas that year in San Diego. It was unusually cold, with snow flurries Christmas Eve. That day he writes: "1) Why do I get depressed after being around Mom and

Dad for a while? I think it is because of my expectations that something wonderful is going to happen, but it never does. Mom and Dad have their roles and they always play them."

At meals he swallowed vitamin after vitamin.

His ice cube trays filled with a yellowish substance called AL-721, which at that moment held some sort of promise.

The new books on his shelf: *You Can Heal Your Life. Love, Medicine and Miracles.*

He recovered from the pneumonia and returned to work, but his health remained tenuous.

As with his previous job, this one required a security clearance, so he remained closeted at the office; I assume he didn't specify to coworkers which kind of pneumonia he'd suffered from, though they must have suspected.

His face had taken on that particular AIDS gauntness, common before treatment improved.

At some point the side effects of AZT got to be too much, and he had to stop taking it.

February 2, 1988:

> Random Thoughts
> . . .
> 4) Did I create my illness?

The eerie kinship between such notions and "don't feel."

More than once he lists "reasons why I hate myself."

More than once he writes that he's a "slut" who deserved to get AIDS.

I don't remember him actually saying that to me, but I had many difficult conversations with him that year about various things that worried him, such as a lawsuit stemming from a car accident he had had while on vacation with Bill in Hawaii.

That summer I visited him in San Diego. At some point he tried to make amends with me over childhood, and I brushed him aside, saying it wasn't important.

I tried to get him to go back into therapy, but he said he already saw too many doctors.

He was also surrounded by the epidemic: as the *Union* reported later that year, "San Diego County has seen a higher rate of increase in AIDS cases in 1988 than any other metropolitan area . . ."

Undated: "fear fear fear"

Undated:

> anger
> being nagged from 6 angles about using antidepressants
> . . .
> memory problems

Undated: "I need to forgive myself"

Undated: "feeling suicidal—afraid to live and afraid to die"

Undated:

> feeling really beaten down—I want to walk around
> with my head down and my shoulders hunched over
> . . .
>
> Insanity: getting an adrenalin rush by getting irra-
> tionally angry about something, usually something that
> happened years ago

The helplessness I felt that year whenever I saw him or spoke
to him—leaden and pervasive.

Of my last visit with him, the week of Christmas 1988, I
wrote in *The Hurry-Up Song:*

> On the way home [from Balboa Park], he told me he
> had begun to forget things more and more. He
> couldn't balance his checkbook. He fell asleep at work
> all the time. Or he went blank and couldn't remember
> technical things he'd known for years.
>
> I didn't understand just how serious this was.
> The old highway curved between lush embankments.
> I watched the oleanders swaying along the shoulder.

My turning away, and my guilt at turning away.

8

IN JANUARY KEN was hospitalized again, following a car
accident. The dementia had reached a point where he was

too disoriented to drive, and he hit a palm tree. At Jeff's urging, my parents went down again to take care of him.

I didn't manage to visit him again before he died.

When I e-mailed Jeff, not having spoken to him for twenty years, he revealed for the first time his anger at me over my absence during Ken's final days: "I felt you needed to be by his bedside," Jeff wrote. "He needed you. He didn't know how to reach out to you and neither did I."

After Ken's death, my failure to reach San Diego had served as the focal point for all my regrets, and Jeff's e-mail reactivated both my guilt and the accompanying defensiveness.

Twenty years ago I had sensed a certain coolness emanating from Jeff and had wondered why, but I had never had the courage to ask him about it.

I call Jeff from the weekend house that John and I now share, so I'll have John there in case the conversation doesn't go well.

Surrounded by knotty pine, I reconstruct what happened in February 1989. It's in *The Hurry-Up Song*, but Jeff must not have read it. He's startled to learn that my mother actually discouraged us from visiting Ken. She said we would only tire him out and delay his recovery. My sister Carol, who is the oldest, overrode her objections and went to San Diego anyway. When Carol got there she called to say the situation was very bad and I had better get on a plane too. She gave the phone to Ken and he managed to croak out, "Come soon." Indeed it was the only coherent thing he said to me that day, so I booked a flight immediately. But when I spoke to my mother again, I let slip that the fare would be $900, which in my parsimonious family virtually shouted the gravity of the situation and thus threw her into a panic. Paul had also been there that week, and my mother said that if I came too, "Ken might think he was dying." I didn't quite put it together that she herself didn't want to think he was dying, but I did see that there was no reasoning with her. "Mom—he said, 'Come soon,'" I tried, but she declared he didn't know what he was saying. Indeed she begged me not to come, and because she was Ken's main caregiver and now seemed on the verge of collapse—I could hear her panting into the receiver—I decided I had to respect her wishes, and I canceled my trip.

At this point in the story I sigh, and Jeff says something like, "Oh God." Evidently my mother didn't tell him I had tried to come. "I guess she was just trying to control the situation any way she could," I offer, trying to be philosophical. But Jeff and I are both crying. A couple of weeks after my attempted visit, my parents drove back up to San Jose to attend to their affairs, leaving Ken alone with the home-care workers. Jeff tells me he was astonished that one of them didn't stay behind in San Diego. Even then my mother told me not to come—there was nothing I could do, he wouldn't even know I was there. I myself was scared of what I'd find in San Diego if I did go. Jeff had a full-time job but tried to look in on him at least once a day. As Ken began quickly to decline, Jeff pleaded with my parents to fly down immediately, but they said it would take them a few days to get there. By this point everyone was acting on instinct, and my parents' instinct was denial. On morphine now, Ken was having trouble breathing. I did then persuade my mother that I should go ahead and fly out to

San Diego, in the hope that something could be done for him, but he died before I arrived.

Is it merely coincidence that I also failed to reach my mother before she died?

As Jeff and I continue talking, my helplessness and despair seem as present as they were in February 1989. Jeff seems equally plunged into the past.

I take some comfort in the sound of John out in the kitchen, making a soup.

I had never actually spoken to Jeff before Ken died, so I'm surprised to learn just how much he did for my brother, such as setting up home care and visits from a social worker, for which I'm grateful.

I try to move the conversation to Jeff's other memories of Ken—how they met, what kinds of things they liked to do together, how he would describe Ken's personality.

I ask him to tell me again about the Tippi incident, which he once shared with me during a visit to New York, and he tries, but neither of us has much heart to speak of happier times.

This is what the story of Ken's death has always done to me.

Though Jeff says he understands now my absence during those last fateful weeks, still I feel culpable. I may always feel so. Certainly I'll always wish Ken hadn't died alone.

9

ALL THOSE YEARS, Jeff's unspoken disapproval had contributed to my perception that Ken himself had been angry with me.

To my surprise, I appear only once in his diary:

> Resentments today
> Cliff broke toy car (1961?) where am I at fault?
> Reliving the past . . .

It's possible he simply didn't record the times I let him down, but the journal otherwise contains lists and lists of resentments.

My fear of finding more to regret: another reason I hadn't wanted to read the diary. But now I feel almost blank—as if I've been deprived of some final argument with him.

And then there's my own disappointment in Ken, such as the childish wish that my big brother could always have been brave and full of love as he faced down death.

I had also worried that his diary would show me more of what I didn't like about him. It has, but it has also given me much more to admire.

In those notes to himself I see a man simply trying to understand his own life and, despite his mistakes, undergoing profound change. Later, as the virus took hold, I see him trying to face in himself whatever he could, against the onslaught.

Not far into assembling this essay, I began to perceive Ken's story simply rolling out on the page, not only in his own words but of its own accord, governed by the neutral laws of plot and characterization rather than by the vagaries of my own mind—which for twenty-one years had been attempting to control and contain what I saw as an irredeemably tragic narrative.

All that time I had hoped to limit the horror of what happened to him and to preserve the only thing I felt I had left: my own, albeit partial, view of him.

But Ken's own account has relieved me of that, as have my conversations with Arthur, Jeff, and Jim.

From this standpoint, AIDS becomes simply one aspect of his life.

I never thought I'd say that.

I remind myself that I may also circle back to my mother someday, and see her life differently too.

A future coin in the glass of water beside my pillow.

One more story from Arthur: He and Ken didn't get back together, but Arthur recalls a time the two of them went to the San Diego County Fair. This must have been about a year and a half before Ken died. "We [each] rode on an elephant," Arthur tells me. "So we got these little stickers or a pin that said, 'I rode on an elephant.' It was maybe a baby elephant— probably about a good five or almost six feet high. It wasn't that big an elephant. But we were having fun. There were times he would just say, 'I have this fantasy of doing this.' So we would go and do something in particular."

"A Memoir of Losing My Brother" is the subtitle of *The Hurry-Up Song*.

Ken on a baby elephant—jostled awkwardly, laughing, holding on—

In such particularities, I find my brother again.

ACKNOWLEDGMENTS

For advice and encouragement from the start of this project, I'm indebted to Lisa Cohen, Gabrielle Glancy, Wayne Koestenbaum, Catherine Kudlick, John Kureck, Robert Marshall, Maria Massie, Michelle Memran, and Ralph Sassone.

Crucial guidance and assistance were also provided by Mark Krotov, Peter Mayer, Liese Mayer, Michael Goldsmith, and Bernie Schleifer at The Overlook Press, and by Kevin Bentley, Carol Chase Conte, Helen Chase, Chantal Clarke, Adly Elewa, Noelle Hannon, the New York Foundation for the Arts, Westbeth Artists Community, and Lauren Wein.

I'm grateful to Peter Terzian for commissioning "Am I Getting Warmer?" for his anthology *Heavy Rotation*, Liz Brown for soliciting "The Condition of Leftover Baggage" for *LIT*, Raphael Kadushin for choosing "Egypt, in One Sense" for *Big Trips*, and Wesley Gibson and Charles Flowers for publishing "The Tooth Fairy" in *Bloom*.

For additional support and advice, thanks to Jo Ann Beard, Paul Chase, Bernard Cooper, David Gates, Erin Hayes,

Brian Kiteley, Mike and Jean Kudlick, Douglas Martin, David Rakoff, Kit and Joe Reed, Richard Rodriguez, Rakesh Satyal, Matthew Sharpe, Bruce Shenitz, Diane Simmons, Frederic Tuten, Deb Olin Unferth, Elizabeth Willis, Kent Wolf, and Michael Woods.

Finally, I owe special gratitude to Arthur Henderson, James Stoddart, and Jeffrey Wynne for agreeing to be interviewed about my brother Ken.